HANDLE
with
Prayer

❧ BY ALAN COHEN ❧

Books

*Are You As Happy As
    Your Dog?*
Companions of the Heart
Dare to Be Yourself
A Deep Breath of Life
*The Dragon Doesn't Live
    Here Anymore*
Handle with Prayer
*Have You Hugged a
    Monster Today?*
I Had It All the Time
Joy Is My Compass
Lifestyles of the Rich in Spirit
The Peace That You Seek
Rising in Love
Setting the Seen

Audiocassettes

Deep Relaxation
*The Dragon Doesn't Live Here
    Anymore* (audio book)
Eden Morning
Handle with Prayer
    (audio book)
I Believe in You
I Had It All the Time
    (audio book)
*Journey to the Center of the
    Heart* (also on CD)
Living from the Heart
Peace

Videocassette

The Wisdom of the Spirit

....

(All of the above are available through
Alan Cohen Publications: 800-462-3013 or
Hay House, Inc.: 800-654-5126.)

Please visit the Hay House Website at:
www.hayhouse.com and
Alan Cohen's Website at: **www.alancohen.com**

HANDLE
with
Prayer

*Harnessing the Power
to Make Your
Dreams Come Through*

ALAN COHEN

Hay House, Inc.
Carlsbad, CA

Published and distributed in the United States by:
Hay House, Inc., P.O. Box 5100, Carlsbad, CA 92018-5100
(800) 654-5126 • (800) 650-5115 (fax)

Edited by: Jill Kramer   *Designed by:* Christy Salinas

Library of Congress Cataloging-in-Publication Data

Cohen, Alan, 1950–
        Handle with prayer : harnessing the power to make your dreams come through / Alan Cohen.
            p.   cm.
        ISBN 1-56170-467-9 (hardcover)
        1. Prayer.   2. Self-realization—Religious aspects.
            I. Title.
BL560.C636   1998
291.4'3—dc21   97-38449
                                                          CIP

ISBN 1-56170-467-9

01 00 99 98   4 3 2 1
First Printing, February 1998

Printed in the United States of America

Prayer is not the overcoming of God's reluctance, but the taking hold of God's willingness.

—Phillip Brooks

 CONTENTS

❧ INTRODUCTION ☙

Prayer is making a comeback. In the face of many profound changes in and around us, many spiritual seekers are turning inward for answers. We are realizing that real peace comes not from importing our good from the outer world, but from discovering our inner riches.

Prayer is the greatest power at our disposal, yet it has gone largely unused because we have been taught that God is an old man with a long beard sitting on a distant cloud waiting to toss gumdrops to a few lucky ones, and cast lightning bolts at the rest of us. *Nothing could be further from the truth,* and this book sets the record straight.

Handle with Prayer begins with the premise that God is a God of love, we are beloved offspring of God, and it is God's good pleasure to give us all that our hearts desire. It is not original sin that we need to overcome, but the belief that we are separate from God, small and powerless. We are the shining glory of God's creation, and nothing less shall ever satisfy us—or Spirit's intention for us.

Practicing the prayer power principles in this book will enable you to accomplish the critical attitudinal shift necessary to master manifestation: We must pray not *to* God, but *from* God. Once and for all, we must recognize that the power of God is *within* us, and expresses *as* us.

I feel honored to set out on this, the most magnificent of all adventures with you. As we join our minds and hearts and turn our vision to heaven, we can achieve our loftiest dreams...and much, much more.

Blessings, friends, on your journey. May you receive the peace, joy, and well-being you seek, and may you bask in the great love that you richly deserve.

— Alan Cohen

❧ THE KING'S ❧
FOUR CHILDREN

Once upon a time there was a king who ruled a vast kingdom. King Jonas was a benevolent monarch who treated all of his subjects with kindness and generosity, inspired deep loyalty; and established goodwill, harmony, and prosperity throughout his land. Jonas was known far and wide as a great leader with fabulous wealth and a huge heart.

Jonas had four children, whom he loved above all else. From the moment of their birth, the king and his wife, Queen Florence, celebrated their children's lives, gave them all they wanted and needed, and enjoyed watching them grow in the splendor of their kingdom.

After Queen Florence died unexpectedly, the two princes and two princesses wanted to travel abroad to explore the world. Although King Jonas tried to assure his children that they had everything they needed in their own kingdom, he recognized that they had to follow their desires. In accordance with their wishes, he sent each of them to a faraway country to learn about the ways of life there and discover themselves.

At first, the children corresponded regularly with their father, but eventually each of them stopped writing. Although the king's couriers delivered many letters from the royal palace, they were not returned. After some time, King Jonas became concerned about his beloved ones, but his advisors reminded him that the children were immersed in a learning experience, and somehow, sometime, they would find their way home. In spite of this advice, King Jonas was lonely for his children. He was also concerned about having a proper heir who would continue to rule his kingdom with fairness and prosperity. On a daily basis, the king prayed for the return of his dear sons and daughters.

After many years, Princess Marissa appeared at the gate of the castle, dressed in rags. When he looked into his daughter's eyes, King Jonas could see that her thoughts were as disheveled as her appearance. Quickly the king dispatched the royal dressmaker to fit Marissa with new garments of silk and cashmere and adorn her with jewelry of the purest gold. But Marissa cast them all off and clutched at the drab attire she had adopted. The king had a great feast prepared and invited Marissa to dine with him, but she refused. "I cannot sit in this great hall," Marissa replied. "I am not worthy." No matter what King Jonas offered his beloved daughter, she threw it back, declaring, "I am not fit to receive such a great gift."

Perturbed, the king dispatched his royal lieutenant to the city where Marissa had lived in order to discover what had happened to this bright and beautiful young woman. After a time, the lieutenant returned and explained, "Marissa fell in with a band of beggars. She wore hand-me-downs, slept on the streets, and pleaded for alms from passersby. She lived with the paupers for so long that she came to believe she was one of them. Eventually Marissa forgot her identity as your child and heir to an opulent kingdom. Now she believes that she does not deserve anything better than rags and scraps, and she pushes away all that she is offered."

King Jonas was quite sad about this turn of events.

Several years later, Prince Jason returned. Elated over this momentous homecoming, King Jonas ordered a royal feast to be prepared in honor of his son. During the afternoon before the banquet, Jonas strolled through the castle, making sure that all preparations were proceeding properly. When he entered the palace kitchen, the king was astonished to find Jason stirring a huge pot of soup. Instead of wearing the royal prince's garb, he was clad in a dirty apron, and sweat dripped from his brow.

"Jason!" his father exclaimed. "What are you doing in here? You should be enjoying your homecoming and bathing for tonight's banquet!"

"Sorry, father," Jason replied curtly. "I must work to prepare for tonight. I must make sure that all the food is ready and tasty for our guests."

"But *you* are the guest of honor," his father tried to explain.

But Jason could not hear him; he was chopping vegetables so vigorously that the sound of the knife rapping against the cutting board drowned out his father's voice.

Again the king was sad.

Years passed, and King Jonas became more and more anxious about his children. Had his other son and daughter succumbed to the hypnosis of the world, too? Then one day Princess Iona arrived at the castle on a magnificent white horse. King Jonas was delighted to see that she had retained her royal garb and looked nothing like the beggar and servant that Marissa and Jason had become. The king welcomed Iona with open arms and led her to a royal stateroom, where she luxuriantly stretched out in her own huge soft feather bed.

"Thank goodness!" Jonas declared under his breath. "She is accepting her heritage!"

King Jonas ordered a great feast for the next evening, and when he entered the kitchen, Jonas held his breath, hoping he would not find his daughter scrubbing the floor. Instead, to his delight, as he walked the grounds later that day, he found Iona relaxing on a bench on a hill next to the castle, enjoying the breathtaking view of the kingdom. King Jonas breathed a sigh of relief. "At last," the monarch said to himself, "a child who is willing to receive what I have to give her!"

The morning after the feast the king called Iona to his chambers and asked her, "My dear daughter, what would you like? All that I have is yours."

"I will have whatever is here," Iona answered.

"But all that I have is what I have created for myself. I want you to have what *you* would like."

"But this is your kingdom, father. I will accept what you have, for I am your child."

"Yes, you are my child," Jonas replied, "but I want you to rule with me. Not only are my material things yours to inherit, but the power to rule as you see fit is at your disposal."

"No, father, this is your kingdom, and I will live in it as you have created it."

Again the king was sad, for he wanted his daughter to be more than a clone; he wanted her to create uniquely according to her own talents and desires.

One year later, King Jonas's eldest son, Eric, returned. The king was relieved that he, too, had maintained his fine regalia and did not believe he had to work to earn his keep in the kingdom.

As Eric toured the fabulous estate with his father, he could not understand why Marissa lived on a little mat under a bridge, why Jason was washing windows, and why Iona simply walked the grounds. The king turned to Eric and told him, "Son, your brother and sisters have forgotten who they are. I have offered them everything I have, including my power to rule the kingdom. But they have become deluded in their travels, and none of them has accepted their full birthright. I am an old man now, and I need to know that my heir will oversee the kingdom as a true leader. Will you live with the authority of a king?"

Eric kneeled before his father, took King Jonas's hand, and kissed his ring. Eric looked up into his father's eyes and told him, "Yes, my father and my king. I accept all that you have given me; I will act with the love and power you have imbued within me. I am not your beggar, servant, or just your child. All that you are is in me, and I shall extend your benevolence to all the kingdom, through me."

Tears welled up in King Jonas's eyes as he lifted his son to stand, and embraced him. The child had become the man. His legacy was now fulfilled.

ප ප ප ප

The four children in this story represent the primary identities we may assume in relationship to God. While we were all born as heirs to a magnificent kingdom, we have traveled to a far country and have adopted beliefs that do not befit us, causing us to live in ways smaller than we are and that we deserve.

1. The Beggar believes that she is a sinful, impoverished, and unworthy creature who deserves little more than scraps from the coffers of others who merit and have more. She thinks and lives in lack, and talks of the meagerness and inequities of the world. She attracts others who believe that they too are beggars, and finds agreement with them. When offered more, she cannot believe that she deserves better, and if she does not outright reject her gifts, she sabotages them when they come.

The beggar approaches prayer with a sense of pleading. "Please give me this," or "Please help me with that," bespeak an attitude of unworthiness beseeching mercy. The beggar does not realize that she could manifest whatever she wishes simply by knowing her worth and speaking the word.

Is the prayer of the beggar valid? Absolutely. Do we all come to God at times begging, "Please help me!"? We do. Do such prayers get results? They do.

Even in beggar consciousness, the one who prays acknowledges a Higher Power and focuses with faith and belief on the object of her desire. Such prayers are heard by the God within, and they are answered according to the petitioner's willingness to receive.

While pleading prayers get results, the element of self-diminution does not honor the petitioner's true nature. Such a person has not yet discovered that she can summon greater help by assuming a position of authority rather than meekness.

2. The Servant rises higher than the beggar in that he recognizes that he has a right to the riches of the kingdom, but he limits himself by believing that he must work to earn them. He does not realize that the kingdom is a gift, not a payoff. When Jesus declared, "My grace is sufficient unto thee," he identified heaven as an intrinsic right, not the result of attainment.

Whatever you believe you need to do first to enter heaven, keeps you from it. You cannot buy your way into heaven with works, because you already own the kingdom. If you never did another day's labor in your life, you would still merit total well-being. If you never performed another good deed, all of God's love would be available to you. If you never went to church again, contributed to another charity, or helped another little old lady across the street, you would have every right to stroll the lawns of paradise today. Trying to buy heaven with works is like sending regular payments to a mortgage company for a property that you have already inherited free and clear. Your money is no good in this town.

We must free ourselves of all preconceived notions of what we must do to become worthy of love. *They are all erroneous.* In God's eyes, our worthiness was never a question; it is *we* who question ourselves. (*A Course in Miracles* tells us, "God does not forgive because He never has condemned.") You cannot and will not work out your salvation because you were never outside of it. The most powerful step you can take to gain salvation is to *recognize* it. Then you will cease to identify with the problem and start living the solution.

The interesting thing about enlightenment is that when you become enlightened, you start doing all the things that people do in order to get enlightened—but you do them from a position of joy, not need. You work in the world not because you have to earn a living, but because you love to express your creative talents. You attend a church not because you fear going to hell if you don't, but because you enjoy the upliftment, fellowship, and music. And you may help the little old lady across the street, not because it will earn you brownie points, but because it feels deeply rewarding to assist someone who needs help. As the Zen saying goes, "Before enlightenment, chop wood and carry water; after enlightenment, chop wood and carry water." The act looks the same, but the motivation is utterly and irrevocably different.

3. The Child of God lives in a domain far broader than the servant, as she recognizes that the kingdom already belongs to her and exists for her enjoyment. Imagine that you grew up in a wealthy family on a huge estate. Everything your parents own is yours. You do not have to ask permission to walk on the grounds. If you want something to eat, you just go to the pantry and partake of it. If your parents go on an exciting vacation to an exotic place, they take you with them. You naturally have access to all the good your parents have manifested.

Jesus most often referred to God as "the Father." (While God is no more a man than a woman, Jesus lived in a patriarchal society, and this was the language that most directly communicated the concept to the people he was teaching. Jesus could as easily have spoken of "the Mother.") Jesus never called God "the benefactor," as a beggar might, or "the boss," as a servant might. Jesus was established in his identity as an heir to the kingdom, and his verbiage clearly indicates his relationship to God as an offspring.

Was Jesus the only Child of God? Indeed he was not! Many times he indicated his spiritual equality with *all* of his brothers and sisters. ("Even the least among you can do what I have done"; "You are the light of the world.") *Jesus was not an exception to the identity of humanity. He was a model of our potential.* Jesus was our elder brother who discovered his own divine identity before we came around to it. He is not alone; many have tread his path and come to know their holiness in their own right. Buddha, Mohammed, Lao-Tsu, Krishna, and many others have recognized their spiritual identity. There is no corner on the market of divinity, and no need to argue or compete for whose God or heaven is more real. *There is room at the top for everyone.* The great masters neither want nor need our worship. Our greatest gift to them and ourselves is to emulate their divinity and claim it as our own.

4. One with God. The highest level of prayer is to realize that the God we pray to lives *within* us and expresses *through* us. Jesus asked, "Have you not been told that you are gods?" This is a very challenging identity for most people to accept, for it confronts us with our power—and responsibility—to co-create with God. We are not separate from God. The Bible tells us that we are created "in the image and likeness of God" and that we are "little less than angels." The Divine Presence is the very essence of our being.

A Persian aphorism states, *"The eye through which you see God is the same eye through which God sees you."* When we reside in a state of Self-awareness, the illusion of separateness drops away, and instead of moving toward God, we come *from* It.

In the Hindu parable epic *Ramayana*, the Lord is represented by the incarnation Ram, who is accompanied on his adventures by his devoted servant Hanuman, depicted as half-man, half-monkey. In a revealing conversation, Ram asks Hanuman, "Do you know who you are?" Hanuman candidly answers, "When I forget who I am, I serve you; when I remember who I am, I *am* you."

While Jesus often referred to God as "the Father," on many occasions he spoke mystically of his identity with God: *"I and the Father are one"; "I am in the Father and the Father is in me"; "If you have known me, you have known the Father."* The master was teaching, through his own Self-realization, that his identity did not stop with his inheritance of the kingdom. He *contained* the kingdom, and so do we all.

శ్రీ శ్రీ శ్రీ శ్రీ

Which of the four royal children do you identify with? At different times we act as each of them. We have all been beggar, servant, child, and king. Ultimately, we are but Spirit, and any identity other than the Light must fall away as we awaken from the dream of separation and reclaim our true Self.

In the meantime, you may go back and forth playing out the different relationships with your Source. There is no need to judge yourself for feeling like a beggar and approaching God with pleas, for drifting into servitude, or for forgetting your power to create as the master of your world. All prayers have power, and you can use the position from which you find yourself praying to gain strength and rise to greater heights. We are on a glorious journey home, only to discover that we have carried "home" with us all the while. As T. S. Eliot foresaw, "The end of all our exploring will be to arrive where we started and know the place for the first time."

Like the four royal children, we have fallen prey to the hypnotic dream that there is something out there that can offer us more than we already *have,* and *are.* And also like the princes and princesses, eventually we tire of seeking love outside ourselves, and we return to our Source knowing more than we did when we left. Some of us return in rags, others in uniform, some in royal regalia, and some simply return as who we are. The important thing is not *how* we return, but that we *do* return.

All sincere prayer is the call of the heart for the reunion with our beloved, our Self. No matter how many years or lifetimes we have gone astray, the reunion is complete the moment we accept it. Let us, this moment, open our arms and hearts to embrace the kingdom we forgot, but could never lose. Welcome home, voyager.

છે છે છે છે છે છે છે છે

THE LADDER
OF PRAYER

❧ PRAYER IN REVERSE ☙

When you pray, you pray amiss.
— Jesus Christ

The most rudimentary form of prayer is *worry*. How, you ask, could worry be a form of prayer? Worry is not only a form of prayer, *it is the form most often practiced by the most people.* How can this be?

Our understanding of prayer beings with one basic principle:

To think is to create.

Every thought you think tends to manifest according to its nature. Everything in your life began with an *idea*. If you are going to build a home, you start with a blueprint. If you are painting a portrait, the model sits before you as you set your hand to the canvas. If you are traveling from Chicago to Seattle, a thought precedes your first step. The notion of something coming into existence without a thought preceding it is as preposterous as a flower growing without a seed to start it.

This brings us to our second prayer principle:

*All thoughts create
according to their own kind.*

Apples make apples, and oranges form oranges. An apple seed has never grown an orange, and it never will. In the same way, thoughts of love, light, and joy beget more of the same; and thoughts of fear, lack, and smallness attract their own kind.

*To change your life,
begin by changing your thoughts.*

Because most people do not understand that *every thought is a prayer*, they attempt to change their lives by rearranging the outer world without addressing the negative thoughts they are holding about it. This is called a "geographical cure," which does not work. *It is useless to try to change your outer world unless you first change your inner world.* If you attempt to make external changes before doing the necessary inner transformation, the outer world will just keep repeating the same pattern. The movie *Groundhog Day* illustrates a very entertaining lesson in how we keep re-creating the same situation over and over again until we change our mind. The moment our attitude shifts, so does the situation.

If you want or love something a great deal, you will attract it into your life. And if you fear or worry about something with emotional intensity, you will attract the object of your fear. *The universal manifestation machine is unbiased in turning your thoughts into reality.*

If you are not aware that your thoughts are powerful, you will spend a great deal of time thinking and talking about what you do not want, and you will receive more of the same, and on and on, until your life is a mess and you have no idea why. You will identity yourself as victim, find people who agree with you; and discover news stories, scientific studies, and all manner of evidence to prove that life is unfair and you are just a pimple on the complexion of the universe.

There is another way. You weren't born to live small, and you don't have to. You can shift your attitude now and begin to think about what you *do* want instead of what you *don't* want. Then, the universe will have no choice but to give you what you are concentrating on *in your favor*, instead of against it.

Worry is the power of creation turned against your own best interests. The same engine that runs your car in reverse will move it forward if you but reposition the gearshift. To shift from reverse to drive, *reframe your experiences to find the blessing rather than the problem.* Then you will become the master of your universe, rather than its victim.

What you become is not a result of what happens to you; it is a result of how you *think* about what happens to you. Six-year-old Tommy's parents were aghast as they watched their son repeatedly throw a baseball in the air, swing at it with a bat, and miss it by a foot. Finally, Tommy's dad could take it no longer. He approached the boy, put a hand on his shoulder, and compassionately told him, "Well, son, I guess you're just not meant to be a hitter."

"Hitter?" the child looked at his father questioningly. "Who cares about hitting? I'm going to be the greatest pitcher who ever lived!"

When Jesus taught, "As a man thinketh, so shall it be," he was reminding us that we must keep our mind on our hopes, not our fears. We must focus on our heart's desires rather than our nightmares.

Here is your antidote to worry: Choose a phrase that brings you release, relief, and empowerment, such as "Peace, be still," "The power of God is within me," or "Love is the answer." Whenever worry begins to set in, consciously and meditatively repeat your positive phrase until you return to peace. The mind is capable of paying attention to only one thought at a time. If you focus on ideas that uplift you, your mind will be unable to dwell on fearful issues. Eventually you will develop the habit of positive thinking, and the worry that once haunted you will have no reality. Begin to master the power of prayer by replacing self-defeating thoughts with visions of your brightest future.

❧ ❧ ❧ ❧

Today I set my mind and heart on a new path. I focus my energy on love, appreciation, and my highest possibilities. Today I claim responsibility for my own success, and step forward with a new enthusiasm to manifest unprecedented good. I use my mind to create only the best, and I draw unto me all the support and resources I need for positive change. Thank you, God, for opening the door to a life filled with blessings.

❧ ❧ ❧ ❧ ❧ ❧ ❧ ❧

✨ DIVINE DISCONTENT ✨

The blessing of getting what you do not want
is that it reminds you what you do want.
— Abraham, through Esther Hicks

There is a classic scene in the movie *Network* in which Peter Finch, utterly fed up with the life he has become embroiled in, sticks his head out of his office window and yells at the top of his lungs, "I'm mad as hell and I'm not gonna take it anymore!" As he reaches his boiling point, this character recognizes in a dramatic way that the life he has created is destroying him, and it is time to make a move toward changing it.

If the life you have created (or part of it) is not working for you, you need to tell the truth about it. You do not need to get angry, make anyone wrong, or yell out a window, but you do need to get in touch with the place within you that realizes that what you have been doing does not match you and your vision.

The feeling *"This can't be it"* is a very powerful form of prayer. It is the agony of the separated self longing for reunion with wholeness. It is the call of your soul urging you to return to your own path and purpose. It is the force of evolution driving you home. Do not try to deny or override your divine discontent. Heed its call; capture the wave and ride it home.

Knowing that "this can't be it" implies that you do know what *is* it. You may not be able to verbalize what *it* is, but somewhere inside you, your knowingness lives. Now that you recognize what you don't want, what *do* you want?

A woman who was going through a major life upheaval told me, "All I know for sure is that I want to walk in the woods each morning."

"Great!" I told her. "That's all you need to know for now; just walk in the morning, and you will be led to your next realization."

The moment you shift your attention from what you *don't* want to what you *do* want, you set into motion a series of dynamics that will lead you to fulfillment. Positive thinking does not mean making believe something is serving you when it isn't.

Positive thinking means finding the good in all experiences, including the ones that guide you away from repeating them.

Divine discontent also grows through more subtle, long-term experiences. You don't have to be hit between the eyes with a two-by-four to gain the benefits of divine discontent. You may be in a career or relationship that brings you a gradually increasing uneasiness that "there must be more." If you have such a feeling, give thanks for the signals your soul is sending you. Boredom is more insidious than emergency, for when we gradually adjust to numbness, we are unaware that we have lost our passion, and we fall into the ranks of the living dead. When crisis occurs, however, we are forced to feel deeply, and we have a blessed opportunity to reclaim the life force we have denied.

If you feel there must be more, there **is** *more.*

Your sense of boredom, contraction, or resentment is your soul's way of letting you know that you are settling for less. While we fear that we may get hurt if we go for our dreams, we hurt ourselves much more by putting up with painful, dysfunctional, or unfulfilling situations.

What is appalling is not what you ask for.
What is appalling is what you settle for.

When your discomfort with the status quo out-weighs your fear of making a change, you will move ahead and be grateful for the motion bestowed by divine discontent. At this point, externally dictated values will not provide you the answers you seek; to get to *your* truth, you must dig inside to find what most resonates with your core energy. Sometimes your guidance will lead you to leave a relationship or career, and sometimes it will guide you to dive deeper into what you have already chosen. Discontent does not mean that you run away; sometimes it calls us to the next level of integrity and commitment. No matter what route you ultimately take, the process begins with telling the truth. On the wings of your authentic expression you will find what you are looking for, which is yourself.

ಕ್ಕಿ ಕ್ಕಿ ಕ್ಕಿ ಕ್ಕಿ

All of my experiences are guiding me home. I celebrate the people and events that bring me peace, and I use those that disturb me to learn more about who I am and what I am here to do. I claim my right to live in perfect joy and harmony with myself, my loved ones, and the universe. I refuse to put up with fear and pain. I step out of my self-created prison and stand tall in the light in which God created me. I open myself to the highest possibility, and release anything unlike heaven. I deserve the Kingdom of Love, and I claim it now.

ಕ್ಕಿ ಕ್ಕಿ ಕ್ಕಿ ಕ್ಕಿ ಕ್ಕಿ ಕ್ಕಿ ಕ್ಕಿ ಕ್ಕಿ

❧ THE CALL FOR HELP ❧

If your heart is broken,
let it be broken open.
— Alan Cohen

A priest and a cab driver arrived at the Pearly Gates at the same time. After interviewing both, St. Peter opened the gates and let the cab driver into heaven, but he told the priest to have a seat and await further consideration.

Outraged, the priest complained, "How can you let that man into heaven before me? I was a priest for 50 years, and I gave thousands of sermons! All he did was drive a car around the city!"

"That's right," St. Peter answered. "And when you preached, people slept. But when this man drove, people *prayed.*"

❧ ❧ ❧ ❧

If adversity moves us to rediscover ourselves and the God within us, it becomes an important ally. Pain and challenge are the universe's way of getting our attention so we can shift direction from loss to success. Such wake-up calls are never pleasant or fun, but they do get the job done. *In-Your-Face-Productions* can create tremendous positive movement that you never would have accomplished if things just went along more gently.

The turning point on our spiritual path comes when we are willing to ask for help. We have been taught that asking for help means we are weak, inadequate, or have somehow failed. To the contrary, *asking for help is a sign of great courage and strength.* None of us can do it all alone, and none of us has to.

In our culture, men have a harder time asking for help than women. Men have been trained to believe that independence is righteous, that to not know everything is a sign of failure. (Do you know why recent space missions have included female astronauts? Because in case the crew gets lost, *someone* has to ask for directions.) True spiritual power embraces receptivity as well as assertiveness. To think that you know it all, or *should* know it all, is a sign—not of advanced evolution—but immaturity.

Another segment of the population reluctant to ask for help consists of, ironically, those in the helping professions. Doctors, teachers, ministers, and other human-service professionals often strongly resist going to others for the very services they render. The rate of burnout, drug addiction, and suicide is among the highest in the professions intended to prevent these very losses! (The average lifespan of a medical doctor is 58 years, compared to 75.5 among the general population.) Clearly, a worthy motto for our time is: "Physician [of any kind], heal thyself."

All of us, at times, need to reach out for support. The tiny thought, "Maybe I need to get some help," can make all the difference between a life of quiet desperation and one of triumphant success.

All calls for help are prayers. As you open your hand to someone or something with greater strength than yourself, you summon the power of the universe, which is God. It matters not what name you call this Higher Power, or through what human channel It flows; what matters is that you pick up the phone and dial. The form of asking is not as important as the fact that you *are* asking.

Asking for help is an affirmation that you believe in yourself, that you recognize an answer is available, and that you are open to receiving it.

The simplest call for help is just that: "HELP!" If you are stuck, lost, and confused, often there is not much more that you can say, and no more you need to say. Sometimes you do not know what kind of help you need, and you are not expected to. Part of your plea may be to discover what you need. That is fine.

When the call of your heart goes out to the universe, it is answered in serendipitous ways. A friend, book, cassette, seminar, or teacher will show up and introduce you to the next step on your path, which may change the course of your entire life. You will be staggered by the perfection of the universe, which answers your call in the perfect way, at the perfect time. Then miracles will find their way into your life with the naturalness and regularity of the rising sun.

ॐ ॐ ॐ ॐ

Distress, responded to wisely, can catapult a person into a life far more rewarding than the one their pain caused them to leave. My friend Sara was a successful marketing rep who was living her dream. She married a wealthy man, lived in a multimillion dollar estate in the country, daily chose her attire from a huge wardrobe of the finest fashions, and rubbed elbows with some of the most prestigious people in her state. Sara had just one problem which, unfortunately, she was unaware of: *She was miserable*. Although Sara's life reflected her lifelong desires, her soul was crying out for more substance, more realness. Sara found her high-society peers boring, shallow, and backbiting. Then she discovered that her husband was having an affair. Sara's malaise came to a head when she came down with a severe case of envi-ronmental illness—she was allergic to the many toxic chemicals it took to build and decorate her mansion. Sara became very ill and nearly died.

In the process of seeking to restore her health, Sara began to tell the truth about her dissatisfaction with her marriage, friends, and the life she had built. She explored many alternative healing methods, and in the process discovered *A Course in Miracles,* which reconnected Sara to her spirituality and assisted her in recovering her health. But even more important, Sara built a new life around the spiritual values she discovered, a way of being that was infinitely more real and rewarding for her. Now, established in her relationship with her Higher Power, Sara is much more at peace with who she is and how she lives.

Like the prodigal son who turned down his father's inheritance, traveled to a far country, and fell into such despair that he fled home and offered to take even the leftovers from the pigs, there comes a moment in each of our lives when we realize that we have been watching the movie but missing the show. At that moment, we look up and ask for help from a Higher Power. Whether we mouth the words or not, we pray with our being.

Any call to God will be answered.

Don't worry about formulating your request perfectly. As Jesus promised, "God knows your need before you even ask." Do not fear that your past sins are so heinous that God will turn His back on you; that is a cop-out, another excuse to stay in your self-imposed dungeon. If you come to God with an open and sincere heart, all of your past melts away in a flash of compassionate forgiveness. God is far bigger than our concept of sin. *God is Love*. Period.

🍂 🍂 🍂 🍂

Cultivate the habit of coming to God *first* with your prayer requests. Too often, our (unspoken) motto is, "When all else fails, pray." Usually it is only after we have exhausted our avenues of human manipulation that we turn within and say, "Okay, God, I am having no success at this; will you please help me?" What we fail to recognize, if we wait to use God as a last resort, is that God would have been just as happy to be our *first* resort.

The moment you begin to perceive a problem or need, step back from the machinations of the mind planning how to handle this, and become still for a moment. In the silence, connect with your Higher Power and turn the problem over to God, *right then and there*. Do not wait until it grows to crisis proportions before you call in the power; the same power will head the problem off at an early and manageable stage.

The feeling of fear is your sign to turn to Spirit for help *at that moment.* As soon as you recognize that you are afraid, summon your Source Energy. Do not deny your fear, distract yourself from it, or lash out in reaction to it. God does not want you to be in fear, and nothing you do under its guidance will bring you any results you truly want. A simple, "Okay, God, I am getting flustered here, and I need Your help," will be sufficient. Fear is the signal that you have forgotten that Divine Order is present, and your first priority is to remember it. Ask first for peace, and then you will be able to see how to effect a practical solution. God is not airy-fairy; *God is utterly practical.* Invite God to be your partner in your daily life, and you will make a Friend who will never let you down.

God's will for you is perfect happiness. If you are suffering to any degree, you must stop what you are doing and ask for a better way. It will be shown to you. The more sincere your request, the quicker and more powerful the answer. There is an answer, it lives in you, and it is waiting and willing to reveal itself to you. Love yourself enough to ask, and God will love you enough to answer.

❦ ❦ ❦ ❦

I ask for help with anything that is not working in my life. I let go of trying to force my way, and open to God's answer. Even though I have made decisions that have hurt me, You have been present—loving and supporting me. Help me to keep You foremost in my mind and heart as I navigate my way through this world with Your guidance. I have learned through sorrow, and now I wish to learn through joy. I am ready to live a life in harmony with Your will of peace.

❦ ❦ ❦ ❦ ❦ ❦ ❦ ❦

ASKING FOR THINGS

There is nothing you cannot
be or do or have.
You can manifest a castle
as easily as a button.
— Abraham, through Esther Hicks

Go right ahead and ask God for exactly what you want. Spirit just *loves* to prove to you that you live in an abundant universe. God has a passion for creativity, artistic color, and celebration, and as you and I develop the prosperity attitude, we become more god-like. The fabric of life is one of infinite riches, and the material world is not separate from God's love; it is an expression of it. Rather than judging yourself for wanting something material, imagine that God inspired the desire, and the same God will fill it.

There are many gifts woven into the process of praying for a material object or the manifestation of a particular situation. First, the answer to your prayer may be an intrinsic element in the unfoldment of your destiny. Soon after I published my first book, I came across the catalog of a growing book distributor. I considered sending my book to this company to see if they would promote it, but I shied away, wondering if the book was worthy. Not feeling comfortable in the arena of marketing, I tossed the catalog in the wastebasket. You can imagine my surprise when a week later I received a letter from a friend, along with a copy of the same catalog. "I think you should contact these people about distributing your book," she wrote. Capable of taking a hint from the universe, I sent my book to the company; they loved it, and went on to generate distribution that quickly catapulted my work into the public eye. The invisible Spirit was working through that company to assist me in achieving my destiny, which has served many people beyond myself.

Praying for things gives us the opportunity to affirm our worthiness. If you do not love yourself, you will find all kinds of excuses not to ask for what you want or to deflect your good when it comes. If, however, you love and honor who you are, and you know that you deserve health, wealth, rewarding relationships, and peace of mind, you will be open to all things that support your well-being. Asking God for what you want is an affirmation that you deserve good. "If a man's son asked him for a fish, would he give him a stone?" Jesus asked. "How much more shall my Heavenly Father give you when you come to him with an open heart?"

Perhaps the most important benefit of praying for things is that it builds your muscles of faith and manifestation. Once you discover that you have the power to co-create with God, you can turn your attention to manifesting qualities of life that go far beyond the material things you have asked for and received. You can manifest love, kindness, forgiveness, healing, service, and miracles. Then you are truly using your power to manifest in harmony with God's will.

After you have flexed your manifestation muscles and learned to create whatever you want, you will naturally be drawn to bring forth the gifts of God. I know many people who have had a great deal of worldly success, power, and wealth, and then became bored or overwhelmed with the empire and stuff they created. Sooner or later they wake up with the thought, *There must be something more rewarding that I can do with my life.* At that point they start to think about how they can use their skills and assets to make the world a better place, and then the great adventure begins! I know a wealthy woman named Erin who was disillusioned with her social life, and one day she had the opportunity to visit a shelter for the homeless. She was so touched by her experience that she went on to establish a hugely successful social service agency to assist the homeless. All of the skills she had developed through manifesting material wealth are now being used in social service. It was all part of the plan.

Sai Baba, an Indian holy man who miraculously manifests objects and healings for his disciples, explains, "I give you what you want so you will give me what I want." In other words, God is willing to answer prayers for things, knowing that such manifestations awaken us to the presence of a Higher Power, which has value that far transcends the immediate object of our prayer.

A Course in Miracles tells us, "Miracles as such are unimportant; the real miracle is the love that inspires them." While I have experienced the answer to many prayers, with each manifestation my love and appreciation for a spiritual reality has strengthened and deepened. Through observing the power of love and intention, I recognize that we live in a universe guided by a benevolent power, willing and able to guide us to the happiness we seek.

ॐ ॐ ॐ ॐ

Sometimes you *must* ask for things, if you need them. Mahatma Gandhi pointed out, "You cannot teach a starving man about God; first you must feed his stomach." If not having something distracts you from peace or the presence of God, take care of business so you can remember God. I have met many talented spiritual teachers, healers, and artists who, because they harbor the belief that it is unspiritual to have material goods or wealth, spend a great deal of effort and energy struggling to pay the rent or keep their car running, while refusing money for expressing their God-given talents. Then they take menial, unrewarding jobs to make ends meet, when instead, if they knew their true worth as gifted souls, they could devote their energy to creating according to their God-given talents.

*God wants you to have all that you need
to be happy.*

The universe will supply you with good according to *your* idea of happiness, which may be quite different from the next person's. Some people's idea of abundance may be to live in an elegant home with a swimming pool and landscaped grounds, while others would be quite satisfied in a rustic cabin by a stream. Spirit will care for you according to your vision, your belief, and your prayer. God will meet you where you are so that you will meet God where God is. Ultimately, you only meet yourself.

ॐ ॐ ॐ ॐ

Great Spirit, I see Your hand in all things. I recognize the desires of my heart as Your gifts of inspiration on my great adventure. I trust that if You plant a vision in my heart, You will also give me the means to attain it. I open to receive all my good today, spiritually and materially. I honor the physical world as Your creation, and I find beauty and majesty in all of the manifest universe. No longer will I deny the good You offer me. Thank you, dear God, for loving me and taking care of me in every possible way. Truly I am richly blessed.

ॐ ॐ ॐ ॐ ॐ ॐ ॐ ॐ

✌ CONSCIOUS VISIONING ✌

What is essential is invisible to the eye.
Only with the heart can one see rightly.
— from *The Little Prince*,
by Antoine de Saint-Exupéry

The next step on the ladder of prayer is a crucial one, for it marks the quantum leap from begging to deserving. At a certain point you must *quit asking and start knowing*. When you recognize that you can manifest your visions simply by claiming them, you approach your Heavenly Father from your true and powerful position as an heir to the Kingdom. The princess does not need to plead with the royal attendants to do her bidding; because she is the seed of the king, she needs but speak the word, and it is done.

Affirmations are always more powerful than requests, for affirmations assume that you have a right to receive what you intend. In the Bible we learn of the centurion who asked Jesus to heal his servant. When Jesus started to walk toward the centurion's home, the centurion told him he need not come...

> *But only say the word, and my servant shall be healed. For I also am a man of authority, having under myself soldiers: and I say to this one, "Go," and he goes; and to another, "Come," and he comes; and to my servant, "Do this," and he does it. . . And Jesus said to the centurion, "Go your way; as you have believed, so be it done unto you." And the servant was healed in that hour.*

When you affirm, you marshal the power that creates worlds ("In the beginning was the word") and proceed *from* wholeness, rather than toward it.

Asking implies emptiness and need.
Thanking implies wholeness and fulfillment.

Jesus was teaching us to lift our consciousness to the place where what we want is already real and given. In this way, we are proceeding *from the result,* not from the need.

The most cogent Biblical metaphor for manifestation is Jesus' raising of Lazarus from the dead—a challenge that, to the worldly mind, seems quite impossible. But Jesus was not thinking with the worldly mind, and if we expect to do greater works than he (which he promised), we too need to think with the divine.

Let us revisit the story, replete with symbolism. As

Lazarus lay dying, his sisters sent word for Jesus, who was a distance away, to come and heal their brother. Jesus did not show up until Lazarus had died and had been entombed for four days. "Why did you not come sooner?" the sisters chided the master. "Now our brother is dead, and it is too late!"

Jesus, however, remained cool and walked directly to the sepulcher. He did not argue with the sisters, commiserate, defend himself, apologize, or make excuses. No "heavy traffic on the interstate," "dog ate the homework," or "ATM ate my credit card." *Jesus gave no energy to the problem, and proceeded directly to the solution.* He approached the sepulcher and told some people to roll back the stone that covered the entrance (symbolizing that before we can effect a manifestation, we must peel away the limiting thoughts that have kept the problem hidden from the light). Then, the Bible tells us, Jesus prayed aloud, "Thank you, Father, for hearing my prayer." *This is the all-crucial key to Lazarus's resurrection, and your own.* Jesus acted with the confidence that his prayer had already been answered, and so it was. He did not fall on his knees, beat his chest, and plead with God to give him a break. He did not remind God that Lazarus had donated to the Jaycees, nor did he worry that he would look like a nerd if Lazarus remained horizontal. Jesus played no games, except the master game: He *bypassed everything unlike the goal, and stayed laser-focused on his vision*. He stretched forth his arm and commanded, **"Lazarus, come forth!"** Jesus didn't pander to the situation; he *commanded* it. Then, lo and behold, Lazarus emerged from the tomb (a little groggy, but intact, nonetheless).

"It's a miracle!" the crowd exclaimed, falling to their knees. It *was* a miracle, but even more important, it was a *lesson.* Jesus was demonstrating that:

Spiritual vision is the key to heal any condition and solve any problem.

The raising of Lazarus further models the truth that:

The principles of healing are lawful and scientific, and can be applied by anyone who thinks with God.

If the observers of Lazarus's resurrection truly got the message, they would not have simply fallen on their knees; rather, they would have stood tall in their own power and gone off to manifest their own miracles (and some did). Most observers thought Jesus was throwing them a fish, but really he was *teaching* them to fish ("I will make you fishers of men"). Although you and I did not physically stand before that tomb, as we learn the story we become observers of the miracle, and we are empowered to stand before the tombs of fear that we and others have succumbed to, and command the universe to roll away the stone so that we, too, may walk forth resurrected.

Jesus came to this earth, not to be a god over us, but to inspire us to be God with him. If you are beholden to idol worship, this sounds like blasphemy; but if you are ready to claim your destiny, it is liberation. Jesus doesn't want followers; he wants *peers.* Are you ready and willing to accept your power to live the great life? Many are waiting for Jesus to return, while all they need to do is look *within* for the second coming. If you truly seek to behold the face of Christ, look in the mirror.

🍏 🍏 🍏 🍏

When Jesus commanded, "Lazarus, come forth!" to whom was he speaking? The answer to this fundamental question holds the secret to all healing. Was Jesus speaking to the man who had died, or to the man who yet lived? Jesus had to be communicating with one who could still hear him—the vital spirit of Lazarus. Jesus could not have been addressing the inert form that lay disintegrating; this was the one Lazarus's sisters mourned, the one who would have surely remained dead if Jesus had not applied his vision. Jesus knew that the true being of Lazarus remained perfectly alive, intact, and deathless. If Jesus believed that Lazarus was limited to his body, he could not have called him forth. But he realized that Lazarus's true being extended far beyond the illusory boundaries proscribed by his flesh.

When praying for healing, hold firmly to the vision of perfection. Do not be seduced into giving energy to the illness or the problem; that is what everyone else is doing. Your job is to behold wholeness, and do not waver. In the end, this is the only contribution that will make a difference.

My friend Pauline gave birth to a little boy who had a great deal of physical difficulties as he entered the world. As little Zachary's life hung in the balance, I went to visit him in the hospital nursery, where I found a very distraught family hovering before the window that showed the baby in an incubator with all kinds of tubes and life-support apparatus trailing in and out of his tiny body. The family's sense of fear and worry was tremendous. As I gazed upon little Zachary, I asked God how I could be truly helpful here. The answer came from within: *See perfection and be at peace.* Suddenly I realized that the family's jangled vibrations were not helping the baby, and I recognized that I could best serve Zachary by offering him serene thoughts and blessings. So I practiced what I call "x-ray vision": I mentally pierced beyond his frail and weak body and made contact with Zachary's inner spirit, which was not subject to illness, pain, birth, or death. The moment I perceived the child's wholeness, I felt at ease and stayed with that energy as long as I was there. Eventually, little Zachary emerged from the hospital and grew up to live a happy life.

Jesus had to use x-ray vision to raise Lazarus, and

you and I need to see from the same perspective to raise our problems from the tomb. When confronted with a situation that appears fragmented or impossible, step back for a moment, close your eyes, and mentally envision perfection behind the situation. Go to the inner place where there is no problem, and abide in that consciousness. Then step into the vision of how different things would (and will) be when the problem has been handled, *and it will*. "This, too, shall pass." To live in a heavenly world, we must see through heavenly vision.

๕ ๕ ๕ ๕

I saw a Bill Moyers television interview with Oren Lyon, a Native American who is the *Faithkeeper* in his Onandaga tribe. The Faithkeeper, following an ancestral tradition, holds the vision for the tribe. He is the person responsible for remembering the presence of the Great Spirit, even—and especially—when others forget. The Faithkeeper's role is as important as any other role in the tribe, perhaps more so. If you forget your vision, nothing else you do has much meaning. But when you remember your purpose, you have a beacon to illuminate your path, and all that you do derives meaning from your intention.

Once when I arrived at a Religious Science church to present a seminar, the minister introduced me to the staff members who were to support the program. Among the retinue, I met a woman who was designated to "hold the space" for the program. While I delivered the seminar, she sat at the side of the sanctuary and prayed continuously for the fulfillment of the event's intentions. While the rest of us in the room were involved in the process, she held her thoughts and feelings strictly on the goal. She did not allow herself to be distracted by any activities that did not match the objective. I appreciated her contribution as a vital element of that seminar's success; she symbolized that we must never forget why we are doing something. No matter what outer activities we engage in, we must keep a part of our mind anchored in our ultimate intention.

Designate a Faithkeeper *inside* yourself. Call daily upon the Faithkeeper, and offer any obstacles to him or her, so he or she can keep you on your true path. It can be difficult to stay on purpose all the time; do not beat yourself if you veer. But do get yourself back on track when you have faltered; your Faithkeeper will help you if you develop a working relationship with him or her.

ॐ ॐ ॐ ॐ

While speaking to an actress who has worked on many movies, this woman told me that the process of making a film is quite unglamourous. "The actors spend most of their time waiting around for the technicians to set up the scenes," she explained. "Acting takes the least part of the time of creating a motion picture; most of it is given to preparing the sets, dealing with equipment problems, weather contingencies, and personality issues. To further complicate matters, the movies are not shot in sequence; you might be filming the last scene before the first, and an actor might be delivering his lines to an empty chair. It's a very disjointed process."

This actress's comments gave me an appreciation for the vision that a movie director must hold. Amidst a sea of chaotic activities, distractions, and nonsequential shooting, the director must hold the vision of how it all fits together. He must stay conscious of the theme and feeling he wants to bring forth, and how the final product will be integrated into a cohesive unit.

As the director of your life, you must not be put off by technical distractions or setbacks. When you feel frustrated or are tempted to give up, *return to your vision*. Sit down for a moment, close your eyes, take a few breaths, and think about what you are aiming for. If you don't have a goal, get one. You can evaluate all you do by whether what you are doing is leading toward what you want, or away from it. Keep the faith, and the faith will keep you.

ॐ ॐ ॐ ॐ

One of the pitfalls along the path of creative visualization is the temptation to play God. *Never try to force the object of your prayer into manifestation.* Like "trying to relax," forcing in prayer is an oxymoron. Because God is the source of all manifestation, our best approach in prayer is an attitude of calm and confident receptivity. We win not by playing God, but by playing *with* God. We are not simply creators; we are *co*-creators. God provides the energy, and we apply it. *A Course in Miracles* reminds us that "consciously selected miracles can be misguided." When using creative visualization, focus on the ultimate result, not the means. Tell God the "what," and leave the "how" up to Spirit. My friend Cisley wanted to create more prosperity in her life, so she visualized receiving checks in the mail. A few days later the postman delivered two healthy checks to her. Unfortunately, they were Social Security checks made out to the former occupants of her apartment. Cisley succeeded in manifesting the means, but not the result. She would have done better to adopt the feeling of being an abundant being living in a prosperous universe, enjoying spending her money on the things her heart desired.

If God promised you that you could have all that you want, as long as you do not try to control the way it will come, would you give up your attempts to engineer your good? That is precisely the offer on the table before you now. Jesus promised, "Ask and ye shall receive"; "Take no care for what you shall eat or how you shall be clothed; God cares for the lilies of the field, and He shall take even greater care of you, His beloved child."

Keep your thoughts pointed in the direction of what you want to create, and trust God to assist you. Commit to transforming your life and the lives of those you touch by being a master painter of truth. The palette is in your hands, the canvas is before you, and the most magnificent scene you can imagine is in your mind. Touch your brush to your canvas, and paint with the hand of God.

ॐ ॐ ॐ ॐ

I live in an abundant universe capable of supplying me and everyone with all the good we need. I energize my good by keeping my mind, words, and deeds focused on my heart's desire. I state my intentions and release them to my Higher Power, trusting that an unseen hand is taking care of everything that I cannot. I let go of everything unlike my goal, and give attention only to the direction I am going. The universe knows how to arrange the means for all of my blessings. I rejoice as I know that I am loved, cared for, and supported as I walk the path to my greatest good.

ॐ ॐ ॐ ॐ ॐ ॐ ॐ ॐ

❧ PRAYING FOR ❧
QUALITY OF LIFE

Pray for my soul. More things are wrought
by prayer than this world dreams of.
— Alfred, Lord Tennyson

As I walked through the Marriott hotel lobby, I was jarred by the shrill voice of a woman booming over the loudspeaker in an adjacent meeting room. "And now, as a Mary Kay manager, it is my honor to introduce two people who have attained the Pink Cadillac Level of Achievement. . . ." The speaker called out several names, and a wave of thunderous applause surged out of the banquet hall.

As the ovation ricocheted around me, the phrase "Pink Cadillac Level" ruminated in my mind. What does a Pink Cadillac represent? Success, pride, and recognition, which we all seek and deserve. Yet, I had to wonder, is there more to life than the Pink Cadillac? Does getting the Pink Cadillac mean I will be happy? Is the car what I am really looking for, or is there more?

I know plenty of people who have reached the Pink Cadillac level or its equivalent. Some are happy; a lot are not. One thing is for sure: The Pink Cadillac does not automatically bring peace with it; more often it brings anxiety. Once you have the Pink Cadillac, you have to insure it, clean it, lock it, decide who drives it, repair it, and keep one eye out for thieves and another for someone who has a Pink Mercedes. It is a rare individual who can have a Pink Cadillac and just enjoy it.

From observing Pink Cadillac owners who are happy, I see that they experience joy not because of the Cadillac, but because they have decided to be joyful. I expect they would be just as happy with a Pink Yugo or a Pink Mountain Bike. They have chosen to see life through the eyes of appreciation, and the Cadillac happens to be there. Is there a message here?

There *is* a Big Pink Cadillac worth attaining—but it is not a car. The real Pink Cadillac is the peace of God. It is the willingness to find love and beauty wherever you look, and appreciate yourself and others just as you are. *A Course in Miracles* suggests that we affirm, "The peace of God is my only goal." If I have the peace of God and nothing else, I live in heaven. If I have the big Pink Cadillac but lack the peace of God, I have nothing.

Are we, then, to eschew the Pink Cadillac or turn our back on the "things" of the world? Do we put down people with money and begrudge those who have material comforts? Indeed, we do not. We play with the things of the world and enjoy them, but we do not let them run us. ("What you possess, possesses you.") And do we guffaw at material objectives, criticizing them as too small or worldly? No, we use them to practice the art of manifesting. The skills we gain in attaining worldly goals will help us achieve our spiritual goals.

A Hasidic legend tells of several men who came to a rabbi early one morning and complained, "Rabbi, we have come to inform you that Joseph, Samuel, and Benjamin were up all night playing cards."

"Wonderful!" laughed the wise rabbi.

"How can you say, 'wonderful'?" one tattler retorted. "It is against the rules of our religion to gamble!"

"Yes, that is the rule," the rabbi answered. "But the gamblers gained a skill that will serve them on their spiritual path. They stayed up all night to do something they love. When their hearts turn to God, they will be able to stay up all night to serve the divine."

ॐ ॐ ॐ ॐ

When we pray for things, we are really seeking the attribute of life the object represents to us. Let us say, for example, that you are a professional singer and you have your sights set on winning a Grammy Award. What is it that the Grammy represents to you? The award acknowledges that you are talented, and worthy of appreciation and attention. It is a social statement that you are successful in your career. It draws the admiration of your peers, and opens new doors to greater abundance. So it is not really the Grammy that is important, but your recognition of your talent, the respect you deserve, and your ability to prosper.

If you knew that you were gifted in uniquely wonderful ways, that you deserved the greatest honor, and that you had an unlimited ability to manifest whatever you desire, would the Grammy be that important? Probably not. The Grammy is a symbol of deeper things. If you set your mind and heart on them, the Grammy ceases to be the object and becomes a reflection of your awareness of your own beauty and worth.

When seeking something material, begin by knowing that you are an abundant being living in a universe that supports you in having everything you need to be happy.

When you know who you are and what you deserve, you will attract all that you require. Go for the Pink Cadillac if you wish, but remember that the car is but a point of focus that assists you in drawing forth your spiritual gifts.

Charlie, a man in one of my seminars, reported, "My heart's desire has always been to play on a World Cup soccer team. I am 50 years old, and it is highly unlikely that I will ever do that. How, then, can I get what I want?"

"What is the feeling that playing on a World Cup team would bring you?" I asked Charlie.

"I want to feel the freedom of running on an open field and the exhilaration of triumph," he answered.

"So it is not the soccer game itself that moves your soul, but your desire for a sense of freedom and victory," I suggested.

"That's right."

When I encouraged Charlie to talk about his life, he explained that he felt trapped and unsuccessful in his work. After chewing on some ideas together, we discovered some activities available to him through which he could realize more inner freedom and victory over his sense of self-doubt and fear. He agreed that if he could feel more alive and whole in his current life, he probably would not care if he played on the soccer team.

In another seminar, a man named Joel confided that he was angry with himself for not attaining his lifelong goal of becoming president of the United States by 1996. "Why," I asked Joel, "would you like to be president?"

"I want to free the world from oppression," he answered.

"It sounds to me like you are being very hard on yourself for not meeting your expectations," I told Joel.

"I am very disappointed in myself."

"Then perhaps you could begin to free the world of oppression by releasing yourself," I suggested. "You cannot truly help others until you have healed your own mind. If you can liberate yourself from your guilt, you will have made a greater stride for humanity than by being president of the country. Master the presidency of your own life, and all else will follow naturally."

Make a list of the things and situations you are praying to bring into your life. Next to each item, write the attribute of life the object represents to you. For example, a relationship partner would remind you that you are lovable; a house bestows you with a sense of security; having a child would draw forth your own inner child.

Consider how you can find the same (or deeper) fulfillment by looking within yourself and tapping into your divine qualities and capacities now.

Object I Desire	Quality of Life the Object Represents

🕊 🕊 🕊 🕊

We approach life backwards: we believe that if we collect enough stuff, we will absorb or become what the stuff represents. But if we can discover the valued qualities *within* us, the outer world will reflect our magnificence. Then, the activities of the physical plane lose their sense of drama and strife, and life becomes a game instead of a struggle.

When you are established in Spirit, you do not need to search for your good "out there." Your recognition of the good within you magnetizes all that you need.

Then you can quit worrying about getting the Pink Cadillac. If it belongs to you by right of your consciousness, it will show up without having to fight for it. And if you do not need it, you will be just fine without it. The Kingdom of Heaven *is* within you, and everything else is icing on the cake. You *are* the gold.

Seek ye first the Kingdom of Heaven, and all else shall be added.
— Jesus Christ

❧ ❧ ❧ ❧

All I really want is love and peace. I release my focus on the material world, and remember that as a spiritual being, only the gifts of Spirit will fulfill me. All the things I have sought are available to me within my own being right now. I look within for my power, success, and abundance, and trust that all my material needs will be met in a spirit of joy and ease.

❧ ❧ ❧ ❧ ❧ ❧ ❧ ❧

SPONTANEOUS VISIONING

What you love to do the most is the shortest
distance between where you are now
and your dreams.

— Emmanuel, through Pat Rodegast

id you spend a lot of time daydreaming in school? The number of artistic carvings on school desks is cogent testimony to the fact that many young minds wander to distant places. While teachers have traditionally punished students for daydreaming, *it is one of our most important creative faculties.* Psychologist Patricia Sun suggests, "Rather than discouraging daydreaming in school, it should be taught as an art. Each day a certain amount of time should be set aside for creative daydreaming." Then the school system would fulfill its original purpose of education, which derives from the Latin *educare*, "to draw forth from within."

When our teachers or parents scolded us for daydreaming, they did not realize they were dissuading us from a powerful form of prayer. While daydreaming, we enter an altered state of consciousness that allows us to tap into our innate genius. Some of the greatest ideas and inventions of history seeded themselves in wandering minds. We *need more creative daydreamers.*

Think about what makes you happy.

The more you focus on what pleases you, the more your mind will magnetize ideas that lead to manifesting your joyful visions. *There is no limit to the delight and success you will find by focusing on what turns you on.*

Just after I graduated from college, I saw a newspaper ad for an attractive job as director of a youth services center. I was so excited about this opportunity that I began to imagine what I would do in the position. I wrote notes and project outlines and played with ideas of unique activities I could develop. By the time I went to the job interview, I had an entire program planned out that impressed the board of directors. I was given the job over another candidate by a vote of 5–4. I now realize that I landed that job because I was so excited about it; my playful fantasies led to practical results!

Enthusiasm generates creativity, the seed of success.

ॐ ॐ ॐ ॐ

Two key elements underlie manifestation:

$$\mathcal{D}esire + \mathcal{B}elief = \mathcal{R}esults$$

Desire is the engine that drives spontaneous visioning. When an idea ignites your spirit, you are naturally drawn to hold it in your consciousness. If you aren't excited about an idea, don't waste your time on it. The word *enthusiasm* derives from the Greek word *entheos,* which translates to "in God." When you are enthusiastic, you are linked with the Divine. Joy is the pipeline to paradise, and if you keep your channel open and flowing, you will bring heaven to earth.

Belief is the track upon which the engine of desire drives. You can want something enormously, but if you don't believe that it will happen, you severely limit your possibility to attain it. Your track of belief must run all the way from where you are to where you want to be, or else your train will run astray. *You must want what you believe in, and believe in what you want.*

The key to prosperous living is self-expression. Those who are true to themselves are the happiest and most successful.

Stay open to spontaneous inspiration, for your real self speaks most authoritatively when you are relaxed and in tune with your own energy.

Children are happier than adults because their minds are not gunked up with the notion that they must follow a format or do things the way others have done them. Fear of failure is learned, as is the belief that we must figure everything out before we can do it. To unleash our full potential as creators, we must return to the innocence of fantasy.

Outlandish ideas move the world ahead far more rapidly and powerfully than logical steps. Most great inventions are the result of unreasonable thinking. Albert Einstein shocked his students when he announced, "I have not arrived at my understanding of the universe by means of my rational mind." Even René Descartes, credited as the father of modern science, did not gain his insight through conventional thought. In the midst of a high fever, Descartes had a vision of the formula for the scientific method. The rest is history. Later Linus Pauling (the only man to win Nobel Prizes in two different categories—chemistry and peace) noted, "The best way to have a good idea is to have lots of ideas." Your imagination is the playground in which your prayers mature through joyful exercise. Let your mind dance in a world beyond the obvious, and you will access a cache of treasures more glorious than those of the world's wealthiest billionaire.

ॐ ॐ ॐ ॐ

When you begin to delightfully fantasize about something you want, *you set into motion a wave of energy that calls that situation into reality*. Most artists, writers, and musicians attest to the fact that their best work flows when they are experimenting with interesting ideas in a mild trance state. Contrast this with someone who rigidly tries to force creative ideas to the fore of his or her consciousness—it cannot be done. Real creation requires relaxation, trust, and receptivity.

While you cannot force spontaneous visioning, you can make space for it. Each day set aside a short period (10 to 20 minutes) to kick back and allow your mind to play. Choose a time and place in which you will be free of interruptions, and let yourself unwind. Find a quiet spot in nature, listen to some music, stretch out in a hot tub, or do whatever gets you out of your head and into your heart. Then close your eyes, take a few deep breaths, and let your mind play with ideas that lift you. Entertain only the visions you find expansive. If any negative or worrisome notions intrude, remind yourself, "This is my creative playtime," and return to the realm of stimulating vision. Let your mind wander down any avenue that leads you to greater aliveness. You will be amazed by how good you feel, and how miraculously your ideas become manifested. Fifteen minutes of creative visioning is worth far more than many hours of feverish effort.

When you have completed your visioning, write down your ideas. Do not judge or censor what comes forth. No matter how far-fetched or unreasonable they seem, bring your visions into the light. Play with prose, poetry, outlines, cartoons, or doodles. This method is meant to be *fun*. If you get into editing, evaluating, or any form of judgment, you will strangle the creative flow. Imagine that no one else will ever see what you are recording. If, at a later date, you wish to show someone, you may, but for now, remember that *this is all for you*. Then each day take out your list and read it. See which ideas grab your attention. You will find that over a period of time, some of your ideas will begin to seem very attainable, and you will find yourself thinking of ways to manifest them. Then you will have drawn heaven to earth by your willingness to receive it.

ॐ ॐ ॐ ॐ

Thank you, God, for the ideas You place in my mind and heart. I am open and receptive to embrace the visions You would have me manifest. I let go of my adopted limits and open myself to be a vessel through which great ideas, love, and healing can come to life. Within me now are the answers to all my questions. I trust You to give me the power and the means to accomplish any idea You would have me manifest. I go forth with a mighty confidence that all the good I seek is available and already done.

ॐ ॐ ॐ ॐ ॐ ॐ ॐ

THE ATTITUDE OF GRATITUDE

Love cannot be far behind a grateful heart and thankful mind.
— A Course in Miracles

A samurai warrior went to a Zen master for instruction. "Please," the huge man entreated, "teach me about heaven and hell."

The master scowled at the swordsman, then broke into mocking laughter. "*Me*? Teach *you* about heaven and hell? I wouldn't waste a moment trying to impress the brain of an overweight ignoramus like you! How dare a fool like you ask me for such a lofty insight?"

Upon hearing these words, the samurai grew furious. Enraged, his face flushed and he drew his sword to chop off the teacher's head. Just as he was about to strike, the master raised a hand and calmly noted, "That, sir, is hell."

When he realized the profundity of this lesson, the samurai's face relaxed and he dropped his sword. He had been taught in a very graphic way that we make our own hell by indulging in anger and resentment. Immediately he fell to his knees and prostrated himself at the master's feet. When he looked up, the sage was smiling.

"And that, sir," the teacher noted, "is heaven."

ॐ ॐ ॐ ॐ

Appreciation is the highest form of prayer, for it acknowledges the presence of good wherever you shine the light of your thankful thoughts. Gratitude incorporates both the heart and mind, and instantly paves the shortest road to happiness.

If you practice gratitude sincerely and consistently, you can bypass all other forms of prayer and set your feet upon the lawns of heaven even as you walk the earth. What more is heaven than a thankful spirit?

Appreciation is much more than a simple rote act; it is a consciousness to be maintained above all else. The power of gratitude derives from the most elementary law of metaphysics:

You will receive more of whatever you concentrate on.

When you give thanks for something, you are focusing attention on what moves your soul, and the Law of Attraction will draw more of the same into your experience. By the same token, when you complain about what you don't want, you draw more of *that* into your experience. Curse what you see and you will live in a world of pain; give thanks, and you will find more to be thankful about. The choice is yours.

❦ ❦ ❦ ❦

Harold Arlen was paralyzed when his single-engine airplane crashed into high-tension electric wires. Narrowly surviving, Harold lay in a hospital bed for a long time, paralyzed except for the little finger on his right hand. Forlorn and miserable, Harold spent most of his time bemoaning his predicament and feeling sorry for himself. Then one day Harold decided to give his attention to the finger he *could* use instead of the rest of his body that he could not. He developed a simple communication system with his family at his bedside, using one finger movement to indicate yes, and another for no. Later Harold went on to point to the letters of the alphabet and formulate whole words and sentences. As Harold began to appreciate the use of his finger, he felt considerably happier. Soon, to his delight, he discovered that he could move another finger, then another, and another. As he gained more and more mobility in his body, Harold learned to bless and praise what *was* working, instead of lamenting what wasn't. Eventually, through prayer, praise, and practice, Harold regained use of his entire body. But even more important, he always remembered the turning point when he chose to appreciate what was good. Later, Harold declared that this "accident" gave him a whole new understanding of the power of his mind, which he now employs in all aspects of his life.

If you should feel depressed or begin to pity yourself, the fastest way to restore your vitality is to go on an "appreciation rampage." Write, speak, and mentally note anything that comes to mind that you are thankful for. To edify your thanksgiving consciousness, at the end of each day write down the good things that happened. Be sure to include the "little" things (which are not so little), such as seeing a bird feeding its young, or receiving a sincere compliment from a friend. Soon you will realize that, no matter what else has happened, your day has been filled with blessings and miracles.

ॐ ॐ ॐ ॐ

One of the most powerful ways to expand your attitude of gratitude is to *bless the good that befalls others*. The ego tends to begrudge the good that others receive, as we feel envious or "less than" because they received something we wanted. Yet even a little reflection will show how self-defeating this attitude is. No one else's good can take away from yours; the happiness of another can only add to your own. We act as if there were only so much love, money, or blessings in the universe, and when someone else receives something wonderful, our chances are diminished. *It is exactly the opposite*. Because everyone and everything you see is a reflection of your own consciousness, *the good of another IS your own*. The fact that a particular person and his or her experience is in your field of awareness means that you are capable of creating the same for yourself, and you are probably close to it. Instead of cursing another as a detractor from your good, bless this person as a harbinger of your own miracles.

You spot it, you got it.

When you discover the far-reaching benefits of praising your good and that of others, the practice will become the greatest meditation of a lifetime. You will feel happier, others will want to be in your company and support you, and you will daily expand your sense of gratitude. One day you will recognize that *you never really had anything to complain about in the first place.* Then, every day of your life will be a heartfelt prayer of thanks to your Creator.

❧ ❧ ❧ ❧

Thank you, God, for all the wondrous blessings you have bestowed upon me. You have created an abundant, prosperous, miraculous universe, and You have given me everything I need to be happy. I celebrate all the good things in my life, and I find joy in the good that befalls others. I am grateful for the blessings I see and those yet to come. All is well, and I am greatly loved.

❧ ❧ ❧ ❧ ❧ ❧ ❧ ❧

✌ THE GOLDEN SILENCE ✌

The only true voice of God is silence.
— Herman Melville

My friend Jerry attended a contemplative retreat in Assisi, Italy, the home of St. Francis. The program, Jerry explained, was founded in silence, with little verbal discussion. One of the rules of the retreat was, "Do not speak unless what you have to say is more powerful than the silence."

All the words and thoughts we use in prayer or meditation ultimately lead to the place beyond words and thoughts. Words exist in duality; every word you utter automatically implies its opposite. God exists beyond all opposites in a place of perfect oneness. Although you may point to God with words, you can reach God only in silence. To enter the temple of peace, we must leave behind anything that begs contradiction.

Prayer is talking to God, while meditation is listening to God. To reach out to God is the highest potential of our humanness, but to hear the voice of God is the hallmark of our divinity. As we empty ourselves of the fears and entanglements we have adopted from the world, we rise to become one with the God whose essence we embody.

It is said that "the eye through which you see God is the same eye through which God sees you." In meditation we draw nigh unto God until we remember our Self. The ocean became the wave, and now the wave becomes the ocean. The lover merges into the beloved, and both disappear into pure love.

Words are not the goal of your prayer practice; they are but vessels to be used and then released. Buddha spoke of a voyager crossing a river with a raft. "When you have arrived at the other side of the river," Buddha explained, "you must leave the raft behind." You would only burden yourself by attempting to carry the raft on your back as you continue your journey up the mountain.

Uplifting words or thoughts carry us from the river bank of fear to the bank of love. To ascend to the mountaintop of peace, we must rise beyond the words. Anything in form has value only if it points to the divine. As the Zen master advised, "The finger pointing at the moon is not the moon." Words are the runway to the stars; do not stop until you are soaring.

Prayer is talking to God, and meditation is listening to God. Let the world go, and relax into a silence more sublime than the most poetic epithet; serenity bespeaks an eloquence that words can only reflect. Even the most noble words but dance around the truth. When you have heard the voice of peace sing its silent song within your heart, you will never again place your faith in language.

Many spiritual masters teach through silence. Some gurus live in quietude for a lifetime and bestow peace through their being. The great Indian sage Meher Baba (who coined the phrase, "Don't worry, be happy") did not utter a word during the last 40 years of his life. In his silence, he exuded love and caring that changed the lives of many thousands. I saw a film of Meher Baba's visit to America in the 1950s. Hundreds of people formed a long line, and each filed forward to greet Baba, who simply looked into their eyes and gave them a strong, sincere hug. This was his teaching. Each person walked away feeling healed, whole, and happy. All without a word.

Within you lives a silent master—one who teaches not by verse, but by peace. People recognize you not by the words you are saying, but by the music your soul is playing. You can lie with your words, but your being is always speaking the truth. Ralph Waldo Emerson noted, "Who you are speaks to me so loudly, I cannot hear what you are saying." Let your true self come forth, and words will be your servants, not your master.

Acquaint yourself with your silent inner power, and you will discover a universe far more vast than the one the senses show you. Jesus proclaimed, "Man does not live by bread alone, but by every word that proceeds from the mouth of God." The word of God is not composed of letters, but light. Enter the sanctuary of your soul, and drink deep of the divine nectar. As you allow the peace of God to seep into the essence of your being, you will be transformed into a being of effulgent light.

☙ ☙ ☙ ☙

Before acting, compose your soul in the temple of silence. Before you talk to another person about an important matter, talk to God. Only when you step into the Divine Presence can you act effectively. In the traditional Quaker meeting, which has no fixed format, the congregation sits in silent meditation until someone is moved from within to speak. The rule is that you do not speak unless what you have to say is so compelling that you are literally bursting—"quaking"—to speak.

Take time regularly to bask in the inner silence. Sit quietly, listen to a violin concerto, or gaze upon a flowing stream. Free yourself of the tyranny of the thinking mind, and take refuge in spiritual stillness. Go beyond prayer into oneness with God. Rather than praying *to* God, establish your being *in* God. Hasten to the abode of serenity where all questions dissolve into Self-Remembrance, and all conflicts melt in the surety of the Eternal Presence.

You have heard enough words, prostrated yourself before gurus true and false, and sought salvation in myriad forms. Now let go of all searching, and claim the riches that await in your inner spiritual treasure house. Not only is the Kingdom of Heaven within you; the Kingdom of Heaven *is* you. In you is all of creation fulfilled, and God's glory made manifest. Put aside all the toys of earth, including its marvelous yet limited language, and remember the language you knew before your lips uttered their first syllable. Child of God, come home to your silent self, and complete the journey that never began.

> He who knows, does not say;
> he who says, does not know.
> — Lao Tsu, from the *Tao te Ching*

ॐ ॐ ॐ ॐ

Today I find God within me. I put aside the distractions of words, and come home to pure peace. Within my heart stands a temple of quietude where I am nourished and healed. I rise above human conversation and drink deeply of the stream of my inner knowing-ness. I expand beyond all that I have been taught, and I remember what I know. Within my soul is the wisdom of the universe, and I commune with it now. I am one with all that is whole, and I claim peace. Thank you, Great Spirit, for guiding me home to myself.

ॐ ॐ ॐ ॐ ॐ ॐ ॐ ॐ

THE PILLARS
OF PRAYER

❧ THE POWER OF ☙
A SINCERE HEART

When you pray, think. Think well what
you're saying, and make your thoughts into
things that are solid. In that way, your
prayers will have strength, and that
strength will become a part of you
in body, mind, and spirit.
— Walter Pidgeon's character
in the film *How Green Was My Valley*

An angel seeking to earn his permanent wings was given the mission of finding the person on earth whose prayers had the greatest power to reach heaven. The angel searched for a long time—so long, in fact, that his elders wondered what had become of him. Finally, the young angel returned with this report: "I circled the entire world and found many people reciting rote prayers without feeling or conviction. Many prayed so that others would see them; others prayed for things to fulfill worldly addictions; and some prayed to be victorious over others.

Just as I was about to give up, I heard the sobbing of a little boy in a poor section of a big city. Through his tears he was reciting, *"A, B, C...,"* and so on through the alphabet. As I drew close to him, I heard him praying, *"Dear God, I do not know how to read and I cannot recite from the prayer book, but I love you with all my heart. You take these letters and form them into words that are pleasing to you."*

The angel was given his wings.

❦ ❦ ❦ ❦

The most powerful prayer is not the longest, but the simplest. God is not impressed by fancy words, or cajoled by dense rhetoric. Jesus taught, "Do not be like the Publicans who utter long prayers in front of others to impress them with false piety. Instead, go into the closet and pray in secret; your Heavenly Father will hear your private prayers and reward you openly." If your prayer comes from your heart, your communication is sent and received in one holy instant, and your answer will be manifested quickly.

To offer a prayer that will reach heaven and the heart of God:

Keep it simple. Keep it pure. Keep it you.

A Jewish cobbler told his rabbi, "Most of my customers are men who work every day and drop their boots off to me for repair overnight. I often stay up all night to get my customers' boots ready for them in the morning. Sometimes I am so tired that I do not say the morning prayer. Other times I pray quickly so I will have time to work. Other times my heart just sighs, "How I wish I had the time and energy to say my prayer."

"If I were God," the rabbi answered, "I would value that sigh more than the prayer."

Our devotion is real not for the rituals we perform, but for the presence we bring to our actions. We may lead a busy lifestyle, but if our soul is connected with Spirit, our daily activities become communion. Throughout your day, say hello to God from time to time. Lovers call each other several times a day just to hear each other's voices. I used to call a girlfriend who had a pager. I would punch in the numbers equivalent to the letters, "I love you," or other romantic phrases she would decipher. Those brief messages were the highlights of our days when we were apart. Give God a heartfelt call regularly throughout your day, and your love affair with Spirit will bloom in the most wondrous ways.

The best way to connect with God is the way that works for you.

You have every right (and ultimately, a responsibility) to formulate your own prayers. A prayer book is not an end unto itself, but is best used for inspiration, as a starting point. When I first learned to cook, I used menus from a cookbook. When I felt more adept, I created my own recipes. Ultimately, I found that my own recipes were more interesting, fun, and successful than other people's formulas. Your relationship with God is as unique as you are. Why copy another's method? Depending on a prayer book alone is like sending only preprinted greeting cards to your beloved. When you really care about someone, you write a personal note in your own words. God is moved more by words from your heart than from your intellect.

You may talk to God as your father, mother, lover, friend, or agent. You may thank God, ask God for help, just think aloud, kick ideas around, or even yell at God. Once I was so frustrated that I wrote God an angry letter, telling Him all the things I was mad about. The letter got results; the next day everything changed. I don't believe for a moment that God was intimidated by my wrath, nor did I believe He would punish me—those are projections of human responses onto a Being far beyond personal emotional reaction. God heard my sincerity, but even more important, *I* heard my sincerity. I needed to become clear that I deserved better, and the moment I recognized my greater worth, the universe rearranged itself to mirror my expanded vision. God translates all communications into calls for love. Speak to God heart to heart, soul to soul. Even more than you are searching for God, God is searching for you..

ॐ ॐ ॐ ॐ

Beloved God, I come to You as myself. I am what You created me to be, and You formed me in great wisdom and wonder. My soul calls to You, and I open myself to receive Your word. You are my confidant and best friend; You know the needs of my heart before I even speak them. You are the one friend I can always count on, for You always uplift me and remind me that I am here to give and receive love. I am richly blessed in every way.

ॐ ॐ ॐ ॐ ॐ ॐ ॐ ॐ

⊱ LET IT BE EASY ⊰

**It is the Father's good pleasure
to give you the kingdom.**
—Jesus Christ

Somewhere along our way, most of us were taught that we must suffer to get what we want. "If it's good, it is worth struggling for," we heard in word or implication, followed by, "No pain, no gain." After hearing this many times in many forms and observing our role models play out this tearful drama, we developed the belief that anything easy was too good to be true, and we set out on a long and frustrating journey to a masochistic Temple of Doom where we bowed and offered our blood-stained trophies of war at the altar of fear.

Enough of such foolishness!

The notion that pain and struggle are necessary to gain enlightenment is as ridiculous as the belief that war is necessary in order to make peace. God is love, and love does not ask suffering of the beloved; it seeks only well-being and happiness.

If you believe that stressful striving is a requirement

for success, you will import this attitude into your prayer practice and make it unnecessarily difficult for yourself. The most effective attitude in prayer is not one of anxious effort, but calm receptivity. Yes, we need discipline, focus, and resolve, but these attitudes are all in the service of building a consciousness in which we can become so still that we savor the peace of God like a delicate fragrance.

Fighting to propel your prayers to heaven is antithetical; the God you seek lives not on a distant cloud light years away, but sits serenely in the Temple of your Heart. She hears gentle whispers more readily than a litany of tumultuous raving, and loves you not for how feverishly you pray, but for the authenticity of your call. One sincere request uttered with joyful expectation is more compelling than hours spent battering the gates of heaven. Quality, not quantity; energy, not form. You cannot storm your way into paradise, nor need you wrestle for your good. God is gentle, and so, by nature, are we. Prayer is our journey home to our peaceful, natural self.

ॐ ॐ ॐ ॐ

We arrive now at a principle which, if you can grasp and apply it, will entirely change the way you work, live, and pray, and magnify your ability to manifest to an extraordinary degree. If you apply this truth, it will bring you peace and relief beyond any you imagined possible in this world. The concept may surprise you because it runs counter to nearly everything you and I have been taught about what it takes to succeed. Yet even a little practice of this mystical truth will yield amazing practical results:

To get what you want,
ease works better than struggle.

When you are in a state of struggle, you have lost your peace, you do not see clearly, and you contract emotionally and physically, which clogs your lifeline to your intuition, your channel to success. When floundering, your need is not to work harder, but to work *smarter*. "Survival of the fittest" does not mean that the biggest and brawniest will win; it means that those who are aligned with truth will emerge triumphant. As we hurtle into the millennium, spiritual wisdom is becoming more valuable than worldly manipulation. Get right with God by getting right with yourself, and you will get right with your world.

To make a quantum move toward changing your life, I dare you to take what may be the most significant leap of faith of your life:

Let go of the struggle.

Struggle was never God's intention for Her children—you and me. God established peace, and fear invented struggle. Some preachers cite "the wrath of God," "bearing the old rugged cross," and "holy war" as attributes of advanced spirituality, while they are simply variations on the theme of learned terror. You cannot master love by practicing separateness, and neither can you arrive at healing by indulging pain. You engender peace by being peaceful, and you restore ease in your life by letting go now.

Letting go of the struggle does not mean simply rolling over like a blob and becoming a lazy slug for the rest of your life. To the contrary, renouncing self-imposed struggle will free up so much energy within you that you will marshal phenomenal vigor to do the things your heart truly desires. When you proceed from creativity rather than reactivity, you become a positive force for social change. I once met a female executive named Donna Lynn who accepted a position on her company's night shift. While she had more leisure time during this shift, she noticed that the night cleaning crew was throwing away toilet paper rolls with toilet paper left on them. Donna Lynn felt this was a waste of a valuable resource that someone could use, so she collected these rolls and took them to a homeless shelter. Donna Lynn found her involvement with this charity so rewarding that she became a volunteer coordinator, and then took a salaried position as director of a city-wide volunteer agency. Donna Lynn's work was so successful that she gained national prominence and received an outstanding service award that brought her to Washington D.C., where she was honored by President and Mrs. Clinton, and met several past U.S. presidents and their spouses—all as a result of a single spontaneous thought about a roll of toilet paper!

Imagine that your inklings are God's whispers to you—the same God that gave you the idea will give you the means and support to see it through. Then every act that springs from your joyful vision will become a prayer that will bless the world forever.

శ్రీ శ్రీ శ్రీ శ్రీ

Of all the poetry in the Bible, the 23rd Psalm is the great Ode to Peace. The imagery in this lofty opus is a meditation of a lifetime, and if you absorb its colorful vision into your heart, you will find deep comfort and soul-nourishment. You may have spoken the words of the 23rd Psalm many times, but have you ever felt them from the inside out? Let us take each line and extract its precious gifts:

The Lord is my shepherd. Picture a lush green valley where sheep graze lazily. The shepherd cares for his flock with great attentiveness; he keeps them supplied with nourishment, protects them from wolves, and guides them away from dangerous crags and bogs.

We, too, have a shepherd—the Spirit of the Living God, who is aware of our every breath and offers us constant protection and guidance for our well-being.

I shall not want. We always have everything we need to be happy. We are whole, abundant, and blessed beings abiding in a bountiful universe that provides for our every requirement. We lack for nothing, and as we remember and practice our inherent prosperity, we enjoy the riches of a vast and wondrous domain.

He brings me to lie down in green pastures. Have you ever gone hiking in the woods and come upon an open meadow? You stretch out on a bed of soft green grasses, let your tired muscles unwind, take a few deep breaths, and gaze at the cottony white clouds drifting languidly across a powder-blue sky.

This is the kind of rest we receive when we allow ourselves to relax into the arms of God and be nurtured by the presence of infinite love. We must release forever the notion of a wrathful, punitive God, and replace our vision of impending hell with one of inevitable heaven. The God of love consigns you not to a fiery cauldron, but welcomes you to a restful country refuge. There is nothing you could do that is so awful that would ultimately cause heaven to be denied to you. All of God's children will eventually come home. When and how you arrive is up to you, but your destiny of peace is ensured.

He leads me beside still waters. Water symbolizes

the emotions. Still waters represent emotions at peace, a sense of calm repose. When gazing into a still pool, you can see your true reflection, rather than the garbled image ruffled waters present. As we follow our inner guide, we come to a place of great respite. Be true to yourself and you will see yourself, others, and the world clearly, in the light of forgiving love.

He restores my soul. When we come home to peace, we get our soul back. In reality, we cannot lose our soul, for it is our very self, our only real identity. Through the delusions of the world, however, we can lose touch with our soul and live a hollow life.

There is nothing more important than knowing your soul and living the truth it speaks. As Jesus taught, you can gain the whole world, but if you lose your soul, you have nothing. And you can have nothing in the world, but if you are in harmony with your soul, you have everything. There is no greater grace in life than to find your soul after you have lost touch with it. ("I once was lost, but now I'm found; I once was blind, but now I see.")

He leads me in the paths of righteousness for His name's sake. There is a right way for each of us. Once we discover our own unique path, we are on the way home. "Righteousness" does not refer to self-righteousness or religious righteousness; it refers to the sense of rightness we experience when we are aligned with our own destiny.

When I am on my right path, I recognize that God walks with me, and I know that I am not alone. My guidance proceeds from a Higher Power. Then, without even trying, I naturally inspire others to find their own right path.

Though I walk through the valley of the shadow of death, I will fear no evil, for You are with me. The key word in this verse is *shadow,* which conveys that death is not real, but a shadow that temporarily obstructs the light. When we cannot see the sun behind clouds, it does not mean the sun is not there; it just means that we have momentarily lost sight of the light. In this world, death seems real, and the fear of death, in its many forms, drives the world's insanity.

When we remember that God is present and life is eternal, we are free to walk though a fear-motivated world and maintain our strength and clarity. We do not have to be afraid of evil, because it has no power (except that which we ascribe to it). Jesus said, "Overcome evil with good," and in like manner, we overcome fear with love and trust.

Your rod and Your staff comfort me. The shepherd's crook moves the sheep away from danger and prods them in the direction of their well-being. The pains and difficulties of life motivate us to remember who we really are and where we are going. We can bless our hardships as wake-up calls to show us the way home.

You prepare a table before me in the presence of mine enemies. Our real adversaries are not other people, but the thoughts of lack and limitation that rob our peace when we entertain them. Yet even as we find fault with ourselves, others, or our world, our good is streaming to us, and the presence of God is not diminished by our delusion. God is real, and fear is not. *A Course in Miracles* sums up its entire teaching: *"Nothing real can be threatened. Nothing unreal exists."*

You anoint my head with oil. In olden times, wealthy and royal people had their hair anointed with aromatic oils as a sign of opulence. We, as royal children of the divine, are deserving of all that a king's child would have, spiritual and materially.

My cup runneth over. A perfect symbol of abundance! So much good is given us that we can hardly contain it. Look around and behold the gifts that have been bestowed upon you! Our lives are overflowing with blessings and miracles sufficient to share and extend to our friends. Rather than diminishing our own supply, we are *expanding* it.

Surely goodness and mercy shall follow me all the days of my life. Behind and beyond all the petty laws humanity conjures, the Law of Grace *is*. No matter how much we criticize ourselves or each other, love reigns triumphant. Though we may judge against ourselves, God forgives and calls us to recognize our innocence. As we dwell in the consciousness of love, support, and safety, we attract to ourselves experiences that demonstrate that we live in a kind and caring universe.

And I will dwell in the house of the Lord forever. Where else is there to live? Even after our body passes from the illusion of separateness, we return to our eternal home in God. We need not wait until the body dies to enjoy our eternal nature. Even now we can know it as we relax into our true being of peace.

🍂 🍂 🍂 🍂

If you can grasp for just a moment that God does not want you to struggle, but takes the greatest delight in your peace, you are well on your way to the freedom you have sought. Experiment with letting your prayer time be easy and joyful, and then extend your attitude to the prayer of living your daily life. Relax your way into the Kingdom, and trust God to bring you your highest good. Then your life will be blessed with such delight that you will wonder why you ever thought that struggle would get you anything you wanted. All you ever wanted was love, and that is all that God has ever given you—and will ever give you.

When you have learned how to decide with
God, all decisions become as easy and as
right as breathing. There is no effort, and
you will be led as gently as if you were
being carried down a quiet path in summer.

— A Course in Miracles

ॐ ॐ ॐ ॐ

I release and let go of all anxious striving, and let myself be comforted in the strong yet gentle arms of a loving God. As I lay aside my fears and worldly struggles, I welcome the spirit of peace deep into my soul. Thank You, God, for caring for me so generously over my entire life. You have always been there when I needed You, and even when I turned my back on You, You did not desert me. I open my mind and heart to the gifts You so generously bestow upon me, and celebrate the path of ease and delight. I am Your beloved child in whom You are well pleased.

ॐ ॐ ॐ ॐ ॐ ॐ ॐ ॐ

✌ ALREADY ANSWERED ✌

To go anywhere in time and space, begin by
knowing that you have already arrived.
—from *Jonathan Livingston Seagull*,
by Richard Bach

A famous basketball star was asked how he man-
aged to attain such a high shooting percentage.
His answer tells the secret of prayer: "The ball is in
the basket before it leaves my hand."

Jesus instructed, "Give thanks for the answers to
your prayers before you even see their results." The
master was illuminating the universal Law of Attraction.
When we are aligned with the object of our desire, we
naturally draw it into our experience. If we are not fully
in tune with what we want, we may do all manner of
worldly gyrations, and the goal shall elude us. For this
reason, we must get the feeling that *we already have
what we want* and celebrate it, *no matter what seems to
be occurring in the world of appearances.*

External "reality" is but a reflection of our inner
thoughts, feelings, and energies. As James Allen poeti-
cally elucidated:

We think in secret, and it comes to pass;
Environment is our looking glass.

The outer world is not a cause; it is an *effect*. External circumstances are a barometer of what is going on inside us. Results do not lie. Manifestation, for better or worse, is no accident. If an object or situation is in your field of vision, you have drawn it unto you. If you have not accomplished your objective, it is a sign that you have not yet aligned yourself with it. We only waste energy when we complain about what is not happening and blame others for thwarting our plans. The only one who has the power to thwart your plans is *you*, and by the same token, all the power to manifest your dreams lies within *you*. The question is not, "How can I get others to do what I want?" The real question is, "Am I ready and willing to receive what I want?" When you sincerely answer the second question, *"I am,"* all power to manifest the Kingdom of Heaven and live in it while on earth is at your service.

Jesus taught this master principle in a hundred different ways, yet in the two thousand years since he declared it, only a few have grasped it and made it work on their behalf. *Now you can be among them.* Practice thinking, feeling, speaking, and acting as if your dreams have already come true, and you shall hasten them to your doorstep. You can quicken the manifestation of a future event by concentrating on it *now*. Focusing your mind on what you would like to come about (or obsessing about what you would *not* like to come about) is like throwing a fishing line into the future and reeling your object into the present.

Jesus, addressing simple people, taught this lesson in language familiar to his agrarian audience. "You say, 'It is yet four months until the fields are ready to harvest.' I say, 'Look up, the fields are white with harvest now.'" He was teaching his listeners that there is a dimension in which all of their dreams had already come true—*and so have yours*. You need not struggle to make them happen, but open your mind to *allow* them.

Jesus performed his miracles by knowing that *what was needed, had already been provided.* He knew how to shift his vision from what appeared to be, to what could be, or more accurately, what *already was*. The miracle of the loaves and fishes provides a perfect example of the crucial shift from lack-thinking to abundance-thinking. The disciples complained to Jesus, "Master, there are five thousand people here, and we have but a few loaves and fishes—how are we going to feed so many?" Jesus, however, was beyond being seduced by smallness. He placed his attention on what he wanted and established his mind in the knowledge that there was enough for everyone—and so there was. His sense of abundance was stronger than their thoughts of lack, and so *his prayer took precedence and prevailed.*

The mind of God (within all of us) is stronger than the mind steeped in fear. Love, clarity, peace, and wholeness must always supplant fear, confusion, discord, and lack. The power that Jesus commanded was not restricted to his hand, but is equally available to you and me. The master prophesied, "Even greater things than I, shall you do." Thus, we have not only the right and the power, but the *responsibility* to manifest the Kingdom on earth. No more excuses, no more hesitating, no more complaining about others who withhold our good. It's showtime, the moment when we are all called to stand and deliver.

Dr. Robert Mueller, former Assistant to the Secretary General of the United Nations, recounts an amazing story about the day when, as a young man in Germany during World War II, he received a draft notice to join the Nazi army. "There was no way I wanted to do this," Dr. Mueller explains, "so I made up my mind that I would do whatever I needed to avoid conscription. Having studied the principles of positive thinking, I knew that I needed to get into the consciousness that I had already succeeded. So the first thing I did was to go out and buy a big bottle of champagne and invite my friends to celebrate me not having to go into the army." Dr. Mueller went on to an astounding adventure of escaping from the Nazis, during which he was assisted by miracles and divine intervention. It was not long before his draft order was canceled, and we can see that his purchase of the champagne was utterly justified.

When you think, act, and live as if your prayers are already answered, you become a living magnet for your good. *Let the answer be more real than the problem.* Daily visit in consciousness the place where your dreams live. This realm is no farther than a thought away, and the more you frequent it, the wider will you build the road by which your prayers return to you with gifts on their wings.

ॐ ॐ ॐ ॐ

The God of Love has already answered my prayers and given me all that I desire. I open myself to fulfillment and dwell in it in my thoughts. I live with the knowledge that I can have everything my heart desires. I accept and delight in seeing my good come to life in miraculous ways. Thank You, wonderful amazing God, for creating me in Your image and likeness, and giving me the power of vision. All is well, and my world reflects it.

ॐ ॐ ॐ ॐ ॐ ॐ ॐ ॐ

✣ BRING ME A ✣ HIGHER LOVE

If you knew who walks beside
you on the path that you have chosen,
fear would be impossible.
— A Course in Miracles

Beneath the gleaming white pillars of the Greek Parthenon, Aristotle illuminated the reality of God in a way that is still compelling today. "Look around you at the brilliant intelligence by which the universe operates," he suggested. "Is it likely that such perfection arose from chaos, or does the clockwork efficiency of life point to a Creator with infinite wisdom and unspeakable beauty?"

Surely we are not alone. Even the briefest look into the starry sky on a summer night, or a peek into a microscope reveals the magnificent mind and unfathomable love behind all we see. We did not create ourselves, yet there is One who formed us in great majesty. The spiritual adventure is the re-acquaintance with our Source, the reunion with our divine beloved.

There are no accidents; all that happens to us is woven into a grand design we have co-created with a Presence who is invisible, but whose results are tangible. The game of life is to tap into that Higher Power and use it for our own good and the betterment of humanity. Once we realize that we have access to a Force far more vast than any the human mind could fabricate, we have latched onto the energy that will make our life new and change us forever.

A Course in Miracles encourages us to allow God to direct our lives in a practical way. Its lessons include: "I place the future in the hands of God"; "Be humble before God, but powerful in Him"; and "You cannot be your own guide to miracles, for it was you who made them necessary in the first place." The message is clear: *Quit trying to run the show, and let Spirit help you.* If your ego really knew what to do, you would not be needing the help you are calling for. Instead, base your life in Spirit, and a greater hand than that of the small self will take care of the details.

When you trust Spirit to handle what you cannot, miracles happen. After I decided to self-publish my first book, *The Dragon Doesn't Live Here Anymore,* I made a deal with a printer and showed up in his New York office with the text and five thousand dollars of borrowed money (which in 1981 felt like a lot more than it does today). After we shook hands and I was about to leave, he blurted out, "Well, you know what they say—you don't make any money until your third book."

Ginger Root has been used as a medicinal plant for thousands of years.

Ginger Root
Promotes Digestive Health

Many digestive, anti-nausea, and cold & flu supplements sold in the U.S. contain ginger extract as an ingredient. Because ginger is an antibacterial, it can work against ulcers caused by Helicobacter pylori. Ginger creates an anti-ulcer environment by multiplying the stomach's protective components.†

Ginger is thought to fight harmful intestinal bacteria (like E. coli, Staphylococcus, and Streptococcus) without killing beneficial bacteria. The Japanese use ginger as an antidote for fish poisoning, especially with sushi.†

In addition to providing relief from nausea ginger extract has long been used in traditional medical practices to decrease inflammation. Studies show Ginger has anti-inflammatory abilities that help reduce hip and knee pain in some osteoarthritis patients.†

100 Capsules $7.95

Try Ginger Root to ease headaches, quiet coughs, stimulate circulation, cure motion sickness and relieve pregnancy-related nausea and vomiting, reduce inflammation, and bring more blood circulation to arthritic joints.†

Call **1-800-669-2256** or go to www.painstresscenter.com

† Statements have not been evaluated by the FDA. Product is not intended to treat, cure, or prevent any disease.

I was stunned; here I was a novice, acting on faith with borrowed money, and he was dumping a negative, limiting thought on me. But I was not about to accept it. I took a deep breath, and out of my mouth came the words, "Perhaps that is what they *say,* but what they don't *know* is that my agent is God."

The printer looked at me quizzically, and I doubt that he understood my message. But *I* did. That moment I affirmed to myself and the universe that the destiny of my book was in the hands of a Higher Power. The same God that gave me the book, I reasoned, would find a way to get it to those who could benefit by reading it. And if no one else ever read it, I would still have received an immense gift in writing it. I closed the door behind me and left the printer and his worldly doubts behind me.

Within a short time, the book caught on, largely by word of mouth, and within a few months I recouped my investment and went into the profit mode. I was quite pleased to make a liar out of the printer, as I did not have to wait until I published my third book, as "they" say. The voice of limitation was dead wrong, and the voice of trust in a deeper wisdom was vindicated.

There's a story about a man named Taylor who experienced business failure after failure and finally turned to God for help. In prayer he made a contract with God: "I will try one more time, but I will act only in harmony with Your guidance," Mr. Taylor promised. "I will do only what I feel inspired by Spirit to do, and I will not fight with others or struggle for my good." Founded in trust,

Mr. Taylor's new store went on to do very well, and ultimately grew into a large chain: *Lord & Taylor*.

Take a moment now to consider any area of your life in which you would like a Higher Power to help you. Anywhere you are in fear, pain, or confusion is a worthy start. First you must admit that the way you have tried to solve it has not worked, and you do not see how to handle this through your own devices. Then place the matter under the auspices of God, and affirm that Spirit is in charge. If you are seeking to sell your home, affirm, "God is my realtor." If you are facing a health challenge, affirm, "God is my doctor." If you desire success in your career, affirm, "God is my agent." Then entrust your well-being to the Great Spirit, and you will be amazed at how quickly and efficiently your needs are met and your problems resolved.

Hiring God as your realtor does not mean that you need to fire or minimize the role of your human realtor, nor does it mean that you cast your sales efforts to the wind and become a sofa spud. It means that you place the entire process in the hands of the master Realtor, who can work though human as well as supernatural means. Turn the whole situation over to the Light, act with faith, watch for signs, and you will not be disappointed.

I know many people who have an intimate, personal relationship with their Higher Power. They talk to God like a dear friend and receive much peace and practical assistance. You, too, can develop a close connection with

Spirit ("He is closer than hands and feet; nearer even than breathing"). Take the form of divinity that most appeals to you, whether it is Jesus, Krishna, a guru, saint, angel, or beloved friend. Then speak to this being regularly, as you would to a traveling companion. You can even assign him or her a friendly nickname, such as "J.C.," "Spirit Pal," or "Gabe." (I know someone who regularly calls on "Abdul" for parking spaces in New York City—with great success.) Develop a familiar relationship with your Higher Power; you will find this much more rewarding than trying to connect with some distant entity you need a rocket ship to reach.

From a human perspective, you and I cannot see the big picture, and the strategies we create from our limited vantage point are guesses at best. We see from the valley, while God sees from the mountaintop. God's vision is like the *Onstar* auto guidance system, which, mounted in your car, will tell you exactly where you are on the planet (down to the street address you are passing); will give you precise directions to any destination you designate; will call emergency assistance if your air bag deploys; and, if your car is stolen, will lock the doors, roll up the windows, turn the heat up to 90 degrees, and announce over a loudspeaker, "This car is being stolen." (To test her system, my friend called *Onstar* headquarters and asked, "Could you please tell me where I am?" "Yes," a voice answered professionally, "you are in your driveway.") *Onstar* symbolizes the way our internal guidance system is working *all the time*. The human mind sees two-dimensionally, from the road, while the divine mind (within us) sees three-dimensionally, from the satellite. We can shift from road vision to satellite vision simply by quieting our mind and listening for the deeper voice. It is there, and it will speak.

In *A Course in Miracles,* Jesus suggests that we imagine rising through dark and cumbersome clouds toward the light. He invites us to envision placing our hand in his, and allowing him to guide us. "I assure you," he tells us, "this is no idle fantasy." God and love are not wishful daydreams; they are the only realities worth pursuing. Fear and separateness are the fantasies, and we need not indulge them. Join your hand with that of your Higher Power, and you will experience strength, confidence, and success far deeper and richer than any the separated self could ever hope to garner.

❦ ❦ ❦ ❦

I open myself to the presence of a Higher Power, and I place my difficulties in the hands of God. I step back and allow the truth of love to guide me, and I surrender to a will that bolsters me. I am aligned with the Force of Love that knows the well-being of all living things. Thank you, God, for taking care of me in ways that I cannot comprehend. I accept and celebrate Your presence and love in all that I do.

❦ ❦ ❦ ❦ ❦ ❦ ❦ ❦

❧ MAY I BELIEVE ❧
FOR YOU?

Give faith to one another,
for faith and hope and mercy
are yours to give.
— *A Course in Miracles*

Mary Manin Morrissey is one of the most success-ful and respected ministers in the New Thought movement. From bare-bones beginnings with a dozen people in her living room, Mary and others nur-tured the Living Enrichment Center to grow into a phe-nomenal ministry with over 2,000 people attending Sunday Services, as well as a worldwide inspirational tape ministry. The Center is now located on a magnifi-cent 95-acre site, including the successful Namasté Retreat and Conference Center, near Portland, Oregon.

At a turning point in her ministry, Mary was faced with a decision that required a leap of faith. About to launch a massive fund-raising program to acquire a permanent home for the Center, Mary was not sure if the organization could accomplish such a lofty goal. When Mary explained her situation to her mentor, Rev. Jack Boland, Jack asked Mary, "Do you believe you can have your whole dream this year?"

"What do you mean?" she questioned him.

"Do you believe LEC can purchase a permanent church home this year?"

"No, not really," Mary said, knowing that it was a ten-year, $15 million dream, and the church had only $40,000 in the building fund. *Raising $3 million for the land this year was a big enough stretch,* she thought.

"Well," said Jack, refusing to be put off, "do you believe that I believe you can have your whole dream of a permanent home this year?"

Knowing the believing mind Jack lived in, Mary said, "Yes, Jack, I believe that *you* believe it."

"Then believe in my belief," Jack encouraged. Mary agreed that she could do that.

Through a set of extraordinary and miraculous events, within ten months, not ten years, the Center moved into its permanent home. The Center has gone on to succeed in ways far beyond what Mary originally could see, and she has a new understanding of what the Apostle Paul meant when he said, "Let this mind be in you that was in Christ Jesus." This "mind" is the mind that believes all things are possible—even *your* dreams.

❧ ❧ ❧ ❧

Accepting supportive belief is one of the most crucial, dynamic, and practical elements to put you over the threshold of your dreams. *It is also the easiest.* If you put this law into action, you will be astounded at the results and wonder why everyone does not do this all the time. It is the very essence of Grace.

If you have doubts about your ability to manifest what you want, allow someone with more faith to believe for you.

Accepting prayer support requires *humility, faith,* and *willingness*: the *humility* to admit that by yourself you do not feel strong enough to accomplish what you want; the *faith* to believe that someone else can help you; and the *willingness* to have your dream come true.

When I was about to purchase a new car, I called my friend Michael Royce for assistance. Michael is a nationally respected author and media authority on auto purchasing. I met Michael when he needed some advice on publishing his book, *How to Beat the Car Salesman*. He told me, "If you ever need help buying a car, just give me a call." So I did.

After I explained my situation to Michael, he told me, "You can avoid the entire showroom negotiation game by simply calling the dealership's fleet manager and offering him $200 over invoice for the car of your choice."

It sounded too simple. "I have a hard time believing it can be that easy," I confessed. "Every time I have bought a car, the process has been a nerve-wracking game of cat and mouse. I hate dealing with car salespeople and managers. Now you're telling me the whole rigmarole can be short-circuited by one well-placed phone call? I seriously doubt that is possible."

"I've done this many times over many years; I know how the game works." Michael reiterated. "Would you like me to call for you?"

His question put me in an interesting quandary. I usually don't like to ask someone else to do something for me that I can do for myself. I also do not like to duck uncomfortable situations. Over many years I have trained myself to confront fear and discomfort by walking through them. In this case, however, I realized that if I called the fleet manager myself, I would be hampered by one serious handicap: I did not believe that what Michael had told me was possible. I know that *we manifest not according to external reality, but according to our beliefs*. So I told Michael, "Thank you—I accept your offer. Please call the fleet manager and make the best deal for me that you can."

The next morning Michael phoned and told me that he had gotten my car for $200 *under* invoice.

I went down to the fleet manager's office, spent

about ten minutes signing papers, and drove away in my new car—all with no sweat and less hassle than returning a toaster to K-Mart.

In retrospect, I am glad I was willing to ride the crest of Michael's experience and belief. He had no doubt that he could do it, and I had doubt that I could. That was a good enough reason to turn him loose on the project. I had no interest in becoming a car negotiator; I simply wanted my car at the best deal. The whole process was a win-win-win: I helped Michael with his book, he helped me get a great deal on a car, and the dealership scored a sale. No problem—easy does it.

🐦 🐦 🐦 🐦

One of the most rewarding relationships you can form is that of *prayer partners.* Join with one or more friends who believe in prayer, and agree to support each other to fulfill your intentions. Set up a weekly meeting over breakfast or in some other comfortable setting, and share your hearts' desires. Then affirm each other's intentions, and watch the manifestation sparks fly!

Prayer partnership is especially powerful when you have *complementary beliefs and doubts.* If, for example, you have challenges in relationships, and your prayer partner has a successful relationship, she is an excellent collaborator to call upon for prayer. And if that same person has difficulty manifesting financial prosperity, but you have done well in that domain, you are in a perfect position to serve her. *Give each other the benefit of your experience and belief.*

When seeking support, turn to someone with greater faith and success than your own; let their broader vision work on your behalf. *A Course in Miracles* tells us that "miracles are performed by those who temporarily have more, for those who temporarily have less." Tomorrow the tables could be turned, and your friend might just as easily come to you for support. We go to heaven hand in hand.

To facilitate your prayer empowerment, fill in the list below.	
Your Need	Person with Success and Faith in This Area

When you have completed your list (add more if you wish), contact each person, tell him or her your vision, and ask for their support. If these people are spiritually oriented, ask them if they will hold you and your project in prayer. At the very least, you will receive inspiration and encouragement through communicating with someone who has manifested what you would like.

Prayer partnership is a crucial factor in spiritual growth and material manifestation. Use it, and you will move from a single-engine propeller plane to a four-engine jet.

🍃 🍃 🍃 🍃

Agreement of any kind is a powerful form of prayer. Jesus aptly taught, "Wherever two or more are gathered in my name, there am I." This fundamentally important principle applies to agreements of all kinds for all purposes: When two people agree on any thought, that idea is given reality. Be careful what you agree is real, for...

You build your reality on the thoughts

you agree are true.

Agreeing on a reality can help you or hurt you, depending on whether the thought you agree on makes you greater or smaller. You have probably had the experience of feeling not-so-great, and someone says to you,

"You really look wonderful!" Suddenly you perk up under the notion, "Maybe I am doing better than I thought." Similarly, you have probably had someone say to you, "You had better watch out or you will catch the flu that is going around." If you were not careful, you may have started to feel a little achy, and perhaps even come down with the flu after a day or two. The power of suggestion is strong, unless you supersede it with another suggestion *of your choice.*

When my office laser printer began to print smudged lines across each page it output, I called my technician and described the problem. He sighed and told me, "You need a new fuser roller. It's about the size of pencil, but you have to replace the entire cartridge that it is a part of. The cartridge costs about $670, plus labor makes it $770."

I was shocked! I could not believe that a simple little part could cost that much, especially when the original cost of the entire machine was $1,500. I turned to my assistant Noel and asked her, "Would you agree with me that we can get this machine repaired for a fraction of the cost the technician quoted?"

Noel smiled, shook my hand, and emphatically declared, "I agree!"

I called another technician, who told me the same sad story, but offered to sell me the cartridge at whole-sale cost, which, with labor, would have made the bill $550.

I still could not believe such an expense was necessary. I turned to Noel again and asked her, "Do you still agree that we can fix this machine for a small amount of money?"

"Of course—it's already done!" she responded.

I made a few more calls, and finally found a technician who told me, "Sure, I can replace the fuser roller without the whole cartridge." He drove 40 minutes to my office, sat down in front of the printer, took out a screwdriver, and in about half an hour the printer was up and running perfectly. As he walked out the door he presented me with a bill for $88—about one-tenth of the original estimate!

My experience with my printer repair taught me an extremely important principle:

We can use agreement to create any reality we choose.

If you are feeling limited, you have agreed to beliefs that keep you small. Many of us hold many unconscious agreements that keep us small. For example:

- *Struggle and pain are necessary to get what you want.*
- *War is a fact of life and will always plague the earth.*
- *(Men) (Women) can't be trusted.*
- *All the good ones are taken.*
- *The only sure things are death and taxes.*

Because all thoughts are prayers, whenever you think one of the above thoughts, or one like it, you reinforce your experience of that reality. And when you agree on a limiting idea with others in thought, word, joke, or deed that such an idea is true, you pound another nail into your self-created coffin. This is why it is so vital to...

Think, speak, and agree on only those ideas you want to see manifested.

Ask your friends to agree with you about the things you want to create, for example:

"Will you agree with me that we can increase our business by 25 percent this year?"

"Will you agree with me that I can enjoy comfortable use of my arm by the end of this week?"

"Will you agree with me that we can solve this challenge quickly, easily, and to our mutual satisfaction?"

Such agreements are extremely powerful, and they reach heaven with as much power as if you prostrated yourself before an altar and prayed for help.

The power of belief is always at work. It is up to you whether you choose beliefs that work on your behalf, or against you. Mobilize the power of agreement by inviting your friends to turn their thoughts in the direction of your dreams, and do the same for them.

❦ ❦ ❦ ❦

It is not a sign of weakness to ask for support in prayer, but a sign of great faith and strength. To invite another to pray on your behalf is to honor that person and yourself. If you truly wish to manifest your dreams, allow them to be delivered through whatever channels Spirit chooses. Sometimes you can do it yourself, and sometimes you need help. Developing prayer partnerships will not only increase your material manifestation, but will open your heart and deepen your bond with your brothers and sisters.

Be strong enough to ask for help, and be humble enough to give it. If other individuals ask you to support them in prayer, assume that Spirit has sent them to you for a reason. If they believe you can help them, *you can.*

At the end of a long conference, I was invited to be the best man at the wedding of two of the participants. Just before the ceremony, I went to visit the groom, Bruno, in his hotel room. On that day I felt very tired, and I had to practically drag myself to his room. Bruno opened the door, took me by the hands, led me out onto his balcony, and asked, "Will you bless me?"

I remember thinking to myself, *This guy has to be kidding; I could hardly make it here, let alone energize him.* Then I considered what Bruno was asking me. Here he was, moments before his wedding—perhaps the most important event in his life—and he was reaching out to me for support. When I considered the significance of Bruno's request, I realized that my momentary fatigue was paltry in comparison to what he needed. I took a deep breath and dug into the place in myself that could answer his request. I asked God to use me as an instrument of service, and I uttered a strong and meaningful blessing (which amazed me). At the conclusion, Bruno hugged me and thanked me profusely. Suddenly my energy returned, and we went on to a beautiful wedding ceremony. *A Course in Miracles* reminds us, "I will be healed as I let him teach me to heal."

You are not alone, and you need not do it all alone. You would not attempt to push your car out of a mud bank alone, and when you find yourself bogged in a psychic ditch, call for support. The universe is willing to help you in ways you cannot help yourself. Let your brother or sister's faith carry you when yours is wavering—it's a gift to both of you.

❧ ❧ ❧ ❧

I need help to manifest my visions, and I accept support from those who can give it. I open myself to be blessed by the faith of others, and I readily share my faith with those who need it. I claim the power to create my world by thinking and speaking only those ideas I intend to manifest. My mind and heart are open to give and receive prayer support, and I celebrate my ability to co-create with God. Thank You, God, for entrusting me with the energy to bless my life and my world.

❧ ❧ ❧ ❧ ❧ ❧ ❧ ❧

❧ BY GRACE I LIVE ❧

The quality of mercy is not strained;
It droppeth as the gentle rain from heaven
Upon the blessed place beneath.
It is twice blessed: It blesses him that
gives and him that takes.
— William Shakespeare

Jackie came to our prayer group directly from the hospital, where she had just had a biopsy taken. She asked us to hold her in consciousness for a favorable result. That night in a dream I saw what appeared to be a photographic negative, the greater portion of which was obscured by a large blue book. The feeling of the dream was warm and nurturing, and when I awoke, although I did not understand the symbolism, I felt whole and fulfilled.

When I meditated on the meaning of the dream, I realized that the photographic negative was an x-ray. I recognized the book as *A Course in Miracles.* The message of the dream was this: *The Laws of God supersede the prognoses of medicine.* I was being shown that love, prayer, and spiritual awareness have the power to override any diagnosis and reverse any disease. The next day I received a telephone call from Jackie informing me that her condition proved to be benign.

A Course in Miracles urges us to remember, "I am under no laws but God's." Far beyond every law humanity has conjured, the Laws of God weave the underpinnings of the universe. The "laws" of medicine, economics, physics, social etiquette, and all other human institutions are not really laws, but relative realities based on current human agreement. (Even the "immutable" laws of physics have been overturned and replaced within the last 40 years! Sir James Jeans noted that "science should give up making pronouncements; the river of truth has often turned back upon itself.") If you subscribe to a relative reality, believe in it, and find agreement with others, then the world you observe will justify your beliefs. But lift your mind to a more expanded view of the universe, and quickly you will recognize all human-created laws to be but child's play.

Grace means that love, forgiveness, healing, and prosperity are available to us, even though we may not believe we deserve such blessings and cannot, through our human intellect or technology, explain or manifest them. The laws of retribution, on the other hand, draw a cloudy veil of fear between ourselves and the light we seek. Whether you dole out punishment to yourself or another, you will emerge only smaller and more frightened. Jesus declared, "Moses taught you 'an eye for an eye and a tooth for a tooth,' but I bring you a new law: love and forgive." Every aspect of Jesus' short but earth-shaking ministry points to our true nature as spiritual beings and our right to dwell in happiness and well-being even as we walk the earth. Time and again, Jesus healed people who were unhealable, forgave the unforgivable, pulled the rug out from under rule-suffocated authorities, and, in raising the dead as well as himself, demonstrated that death, the ultimate leveler in a world of fear, has no power over the Son of God—all of us. In three years of teaching (by example) the laws of grace, Jesus changed the entire course of humanity, and two thousand years later we are just getting around to understanding the love he demonstrated.

ॐ ॐ ॐ ॐ

To enjoy the benefits of grace, we must practice it. True spirituality is not just a philosophy; it is a life we live. Love, like the heart, is a muscle we strengthen by using. Love becomes real only when we give it.

Here are some ways you can expand the experience of grace in your life:

1. *Receive gifts graciously.* Most people have difficulty accepting generous gifts or compliments. Because we feel we are not worthy, when unexpected material or spiritual endowments come our way, we question, ignore, or minimize them; or we bat them away. Susan offers Jack a compliment on the speech he delivered, and he mitigates it ("I could have done better"). Aunt Martha offers Terri a car she needs, and she turns it down ("Oh, I couldn't ask you to do that"). Bill offers to pay Sally when he prints some of her photos in his newsletter, and she does not accept, believing that if she loves to do photography, it is not "spiritual" to be paid for it. Then she goes to work the next day and complains about the job she hates.

Years ago I received a free airplane ticket as a bonus from United Airlines, and I kept reading the fine print on the award, looking for some catch. I didn't believe the trip was really free until I stepped onto the airplane without paying a penny.

When something you want is offered to you with love, say, *"YES, THANK YOU!"* Thank the giver, thank God, and thank yourself for deserving, manifesting, and receiving your good. Open to universal love by accepting love through material expression; God works through the vehicles of the world.

2. *Offer grace.* A sign in a pottery store in England announced, *"Please let us know if you break any item, so we can forgive you."* Such a notion is startling because it reverses the laws of the world. Take every opportunity to deny the rigid rules of fear by bestowing forgiveness where the world would prescribe punishment.

Imagine a man walking along a city street when a potted plant falls off the window sill of an apartment above him, misses him by inches, and crashes at his feet. There are three possible paths the man could take: On the worldly path, he might look up, shake his fist, and curse the apartment dweller, or even charge up the stairs and punch him. On the stoic or detached path, he might note, "This is interesting; I guess it was my karma to have the pot fall at my feet and miss me." On the Christ path, he might go to the flower shop on the corner, buy a new plant, and bring it to the apartment dweller with a smile and thanks for growing a green, living thing to beautify the city.

When you practice generosity, you demonstrate to yourself and others that you are an abundant being living in a plentiful universe. You can live generously no matter how much you have; generosity is a function not of your bankbook, but of your *attitude*. Leave a 20 percent tip at a restaurant, or leave a few dollars on your hotel dresser for your chambermaid. The additional dollar on the table or dresser costs you very little, but it can make a significant difference in the attitude of the recipient, who may go on to extend extra kindness to the people she serves for the rest of that day. Love, like fear, is contagious ("Choose ye this day whom ye shall serve"). At every moment you are contributing to the sum total of love in the universe, or the sum total of fear. When you extend grace, you are the first and foremost recipient as you edify your awareness that there is enough for you, and plenty to share. You cannot outgive God!

3. ***Make liars out of limits.*** In his brilliant book *Illusions*, Richard Bach writes, *"Argue for your limitations, and sure enough they're yours."* How apt we are to make a case for what we can't do! Supportive friends try to convince us to take the next step in the direction of our good, and we wave away their encouragement with a long series of "Yes, but . . ." replies.

You can begin to dismantle your perceived limits by dropping your defense of smallness. Take a piece of paper and make a list of everything in your life that is not working, including health difficulties, relationship problems, financial needs, job issues, and anything else that does not match your vision of how you would like to be living. Then take the paper, hold it between your hands, and sincerely pray, *"Please, God, let me be wrong about all of this."*

Your prayer *will* be answered, because you *are* wrong about all of it! Whenever you perceive lack, loss, or limitation, you are applying a fear-based vision to a love-based universe. It is only when we doggedly cling to our self-image as a victim that the universe continues to match our beliefs with situations that reflect our sense of powerlessness.

Be willing to be wrong about what you think is wrong, so you can be right about what you wish to be true.

What you wish to be true *can be* true, but you must be open to *allowing* it. You must recognize that you deserve love, healing, and prosperity more than fear, illness, and poverty. You can be right, or happy—the choice is before you now.

🐚 🐚 🐚 🐚

Saint Paul noted that "change can come in the twinkling of an eye." Perhaps you have had the experience of feeling ill, angry, or depressed, and in a moment you had a thought, feeling, or shift in attitude that lifted you out of your misery. Suddenly you felt wonderful, refreshed, and alive, and the darkness dissipated as if you had awakened from a horrid nightmare to a beautiful morning sun. This is grace.

You can experience grace in any moment—even right now. Healing is a matter of *willingness* more than action, and begins with an open mind and heart. You do not have to suffer for your sins, earn a six-figure income, lose 20 pounds, understand the theory of relativity, or become a saint before you can enjoy health and well-being. All you have to do is *let it in.* Some of the greatest saints in history, including the apostles of Christ, were sinners by the world's standards—salt-of-the-earth people with a long history of transgressions that one could reasonably argue would deny them access to heaven. Jesus, however, did not regard his disciples as heathen, but brothers and sisters of worth equal to himself, and he drew forth their dignity by loving them as divine beings. They caught his vision, and in a short time their lives were transformed. *You and I can experience the same transformation right now, if we are open to it.*

You are not limited by your karma. The events in your life have transpired not to bind you, but to *empower* you. History is but a thread we weave into a higher destiny. Your "sins" are not the devil's ammunition for your eternal damnation, but seen in the proper light, become feathers in the wings of your eternal salvation. We are bigger than our experiences, and we must grow *beyond* our karma. No matter what karma you have created, you can nullify and transmute it in the awareness that you are innocent. You are created in the image and likeness of a wondrous God; any other identity you adopt is self-conjured and smaller than you are. Dismiss all limiting notions of what you must do before you can become healed or happy. *A Course in Miracles* tells us that "healing is available to you now, unless you believe that the will of God takes time." Love is at hand; receive it now and enjoy the abundant life.

ॐ ॐ ॐ ॐ

A priest was asked, "Does God answer all prayers?" "Yes," he replied. "And sometimes the answer is no."

Often we do not perceive our own best interests. If we pray for something that would injure us, God's answer of no is a gift of grace, and at such a time we do better to trust the Big Picture rather than forcing a situation we will regret. St. Theresa of Avila noted, "More tears have been shed over answered prayers than unanswered prayers." Later Oscar Wilde echoed, "I have lived long enough to thank God for not answering all my prayers."

How, then, can we know if something we are praying for is in our best interests? Should we stop praying for things altogether? And if God gives us whatever S/He wants or we need, why pray at all?

If you had perfect faith, you could simply pray, "Thy will be done," and joyfully accept whatever God gives you. Some have lived thus, and experienced the immense benefits of such surrender. Being human, however, there are things that we want, and we are prone to come to God for help—and this is good.

Here is a prayer formula that will allow you to ask for what you want, but also allow God to give you what you need: Pray for whatever you feel moved to pray for, and when you are done, qualify your prayer with, *"This or better."* In so doing, you acknowledge to God (and, more important, to yourself) that your vision is not all-encompassing, and in the event that something you have requested is not in your highest interests, you are open and willing to receive an even better result.

If you find yourself fighting for your good, the universe may be trying to tell you that the object of your struggle is not really your good. When I sought to buy a piece of vacation property, my loan application was denied by several lenders, each citing that my income was insufficient to make the required payments. I decided to try one more loan company, and prayed, "If this property is in my right and best interest, I accept it wholeheartedly; if not, I release it." When I was turned down for this loan, I abandoned the project, even though I lost a significant deposit and some fees.

As the following months unfolded, my income was not what I had projected it to be, and I had a number of unexpected expenses. Before long I realized that getting that loan would have put me in a very precarious financial position. In retrospect I recognize that it was a great blessing that I did not get the loan. From that moment on, I thanked God for assisting me in *not* buying that property, and realized that my "this or better" prayer was the healthiest one I had uttered. I also realized that at a future time I would probably be in a better financial position to purchase that or a similar property. So the ultimate answer to my prayer was not "No"; it was simply, "Not now."

🍃 🍃 🍃 🍃

Because God is love, grace is natural. All living beings are imbued with the propensity for life, and if not sullied by abuse, naturally extend kindness. Several years ago a three-year-old boy fell 30 feet into the gorilla pavilion at a zoo near Chicago. As panicked onlookers watched in astonishment, Bindy, a mother gorilla still nursing her own baby, scurried to the unconscious child, scooped him up in her arms, carried him to the gate, and gently passed his limp form back to his distraught mother. Later that year, *Time* magazine designated Bindy as the recipient of the Humanitarian of the Year award.

If we keep our eyes and hearts open, we can find endless demonstrations that we live in a grace-full universe. Prophets of gloom and doom may find all manner of indications that the world is on the threshold of destruction, but visionaries of light may just as readily find proof that we are in the birthing process of resurrection. We will always get more of what we choose to look upon, for the world we create is the one we foster with our thoughts.

Love is the only reality. As we receive and extend grace to ourselves and others, we become the godly beings we were born to be, and the world becomes a mirror of heaven.

🍂 🍂 🍂 🍂

I open myself to receive the blessings of Your infinite grace. I acknowledge that my vision is limited and I see but a small portion of the grand plan. Fill my soul with the awareness of Your Presence, that I may be lifted above small thinking, into the world of miracles. I now forgive myself and all others, and invite the reality of love to be the guiding truth in my life. I bless all that happens to me, and seek to know You through the experiences of this world. I am released from all the little laws that I believed bound me, and I open to live in joyous self-acceptance. Thank You for bringing me home through avenues far wider and more wondrous than I imagined.

🍂 🍂 🍂 🍂 🍂 🍂 🍂 🍂

❧ SAY YES TO LOVE ❧

I would rather be ashes than dust! I would rather that my spark should burn out in a brilliant blaze than it should be stifled by dryrot. I would rather be a superb meteor, every atom of me in magnificent glow, than a sleepy and permanent planet. The proper function of man is to live, not to exist. . . I shall use my time.

— Jack London

I am breaking up with Tim because I want more," Sue told me adamantly. "I want more intimacy, more emotional availability, and more commitment. It's the same reason I broke up with Jack, and with Brad before him."

Sue had ended relationships with a number of unavailable men for a very good reason: She realized that as long as she settled for men who were not there, she could not have the depth of relationship she desired.

But Sue was still roadblocked by another impediment, of which she was unaware: Although she had removed from her life what she did *not* want, she had not opened to accept what she *did* want.

The universe abhors a vacuum; if you intend to upgrade your wardrobe, you must first clean out your closet and make room for new clothing. But clearing out the old is useless unless you fill the vacant space with something better. If you clean out a closet and do not fill it with what you want, it will not be long before more junk finds it way into the available space. In Sue's case, she got rid of the old, but did not bring in the new.

The essence of manifestation is accepting.

Here is an easy three-step formula to bring your heart's desires to your doorstep:

1. Make a clear choice about what you want.
2. Say no to what you do not want.
3. Say yes to what you do want.

While this formula is very simple, many people have difficulty with step 3. Getting what you want can be frightening if you harbor fears of success, or are not ready to own your power to create the life of your choosing. Like many, you may be lingering on the threshold of manifestation, knowing that you cannot go back, but you are not quite ready to move ahead.

You can override your fears of success by *mentally and emotionally pumping up your enthusiasm for your dreams.*

When you want what you want more than you fear what you want, you will have it.

Your job is not to feverishly wrestle with the universe to squeeze out your due, but to shift your energy so that your joy in anticipating the fulfillment of your goals outweighs your focus on what might go wrong. There is no sinister external force keeping you from having what you want; *everything in your outer world is a reflection of your inner beliefs and feelings.* Change your internal climate, and outer circumstances will rearrange themselves naturally.

❦ ❦ ❦ ❦

Are you willing to let God love you and take care of you? Is it possible that you are already richly blessed but do not know it? Could it be that everything you have ever needed has been offered you, but you have not been open to receive it?

Imagine that you have a 10,000-gallon water tank on your property, and you want to water your garden. You open up the hose nozzle and find only a few small drops of water trickling out. "There is no water!" you complain. You rant, rave, and devise intricate schemes to obtain more water. If you are mistrustful, you may conclude that your neighbor has diverted your supply, and you may curse him or try to retaliate. You may go on and on about the lack of water in your life, until you look down to see that you are standing on the hose. *Oops!* You take your foot off the hose, and within moments a huge rush of water streams out of the nozzle. You're back in business.

> *The universe is abundant. The experience*
> *of lack is a result of lack thinking.*
> *Life will take care of you if you let it.*

A flash flood overtook Ralph's house. As the waters rose, Ralph climbed to the roof and prayed for help. A few minutes later, two men in a boat rowed by and offered Ralph refuge. "God will save me!" he proclaimed devoutly, and sent the men on their way.

Ralph prayed again, and soon a motorboat approached, from which the driver threw him a life raft. "Thank you, but I have called upon my Lord!" Ralph yelled, and went on praying.

Then a helicopter flew over his roof, and a chain ladder fell within his reach. Ralph also refused this offer, submitting, "I trust in God alone!"

Soon the waters overcame Ralph, he drowned, and

found himself at the Pearly Gates. Indignant that God had failed him, he demanded to speak directly to the Lord. He was ushered to the Throne of Glory, where he complained, "How can you say that you answer prayers when I prayed for you to save me and you did not?"

God responded, "I sent you two boats and a helicopter—what more do you want?"

Spirit can do no more for you than It can do **through** *you.*

Sometimes prayers are answered through supernatural means, but most often blessings arrive through super *natural* means. God reaches us spiritually by way of our heart, while S/He serves our material needs through the pathways of the world. If you sit around and wait for dollars to fall out of the sky, you may starve in the process. But if, when someone calls you with an excellent job opportunity, you recognize the caller as an agent of Spirit, you are on your way to an answered prayer.

Be open to recognizing the hand of love when it reaches out to bless you.

Two Hindu men were walking through a field when a bull charged them. Raj scurried up a tree, but Gopal stood before the bull defiantly. Raj called from the branches, "Get up here, you idiot, or you'll be killed!"

Gopal brazenly answered, "The Lord is my protection!"

Within moments, the bull butted Gopal and left him bruised and bloodied. Raj climbed down from the tree and started to help his injured friend.

"I thought for sure God would protect me," Gopal complained, dazed.

"He tried," replied Raj. "Didn't you hear Him calling you from the tree?"

ॐ ॐ ॐ ॐ

Another way we limit our good is by asking for less than we what really want and accommodating to mediocrity. Minimizing what we ask for keeps us from being disappointed, but it also keeps us from having what we truly desire.

When Joe passed on, he was taken on a tour of the next world. As God was showing Joe many different rooms in the heavenly estate, the two passed a door that was locked. "What is in that room?"

"Oh, it would make you very sad to see what is in that room," answered God.

But Joe was curious and insisted on seeing the room anyway. God unlocked the door and ushered Joe into a chamber as large as a warehouse where, to his great surprise, Joe beheld a vast cache of treasures, including luxury automobiles, expensive jewelry, and the latest high-tech electronic equipment. "This is amazing!" Joe exclaimed. "Why did you say it would make me sad to see these things?"

"Because," God explained, "these are the gifts I offer to people who want them. But if the intended recipient is not ready or willing to accept a gift, I have no choice but to take it back here and hold it in storage until that person or someone else will have it."

"That's unbelievable!" Joe exclaimed as he scurried from object to object, fingering each excitedly. Suddenly Joe's eyes lit up and he called out, "Isn't that a Rolls Royce over there?"

"Yes, it is," God answered. "Go over and have a look at it."

Joe ran to the car, slipped into the driver's seat, and began to manipulate the controls. When he saw a tag on the door handle, he read it and his face blanched. "Wait a minute!" Joe shouted, "This is *my* name on the tag!"

"That's right, Joe," God replied. "This car was meant for you."

Indignant, Joe challenged the Supreme Being, "Then how come I didn't get it? Every day I prayed for a car!"

"I know you did," answered God, "but every day you prayed for a Ford."

Joe tried to help himself by praying for a car, but he hurt himself by only asking for the minimum he thought he could get, instead of asking for what he *really* desired.

> *You will get as much as you ask for.*
> *Ask for* all *that you want.*

Many of us are too well adjusted—we adjust our request to what we expect, rather than daring the universe (and ourselves) to match our vision. If you aim low on the pyramid, you can't miss the target—but you do miss the view from the peak. If you accommodate long enough, you lose touch with your heart's desires, and when someone asks you what you really want, you can't come up with an answer. Not expressing what you want is more painful than not getting what you want, for exciting goals bring us life, motivation, and energy. To rekindle your fire, begin to tell the truth—at least to yourself—about what you are feeling about everything you do. As you are meticulously honest about what makes you feel more alive and what deadens you, you will clear away the debris of adjustment and bring forth the empowerment you desire.

❦ ❦ ❦ ❦

We live in a world that has succumbed to the hypnosis of lack thinking, and nearly everyone who lives has traded in their birthright of grandeur for a paltry settlement of trinkets. But settling is never the same as choosing, and it will never bring you the joy of being a creator rather than a reactor.

While visiting a ranch, I noticed some very small horses about the size of a large dog. The owner told me these were pygmy horses, bred to be small. Breeders took the smallest offspring of each generation and fostered genetic pairings so the next generation would be even smaller. This is exactly what we have done with the habit of small thinking: We have focused so intently on what we don't have and what is not working, that our life has become progressively more minuscule until we have forgotten that we can run as free as magnificent steeds rather than living in lilliputian pens as tiny pygmies. But just as easily as we have bred smallness, we can breed greatness. By continually focusing on what we want and what is working, we can cultivate generations of ever-expanding success—which all begins by choosing where we place our attention. Thus, we must devote each day, indeed every new moment, to thinking more richly and expansively.

The Islam name for God is "Allah," which sounds a lot like "Allow." When you allow abundance to be your reality, the love of God will penetrate your heart, and amazing events will ensue. Then you may step across the threshold of worthiness and receive in full measure the blessings the universe has patiently waited to bestow. It's all available, and it's all already done;

the only question now is when, and that is entirely up to you.

❦ ❦ ❦ ❦

I open myself to receive all the good and blessings appointed me. I let go of any notion of smallness and step into my true power and deservingness as Your beloved child. I live in an abundant universe, and all the well-being I seek is flowing to me now. I will wait no longer; I renounce the substitutes for love I have accepted, and boldly claim my right to enjoy the best. I accept the Kingdom now. I receive Your great gifts and extend my riches to all I meet.

❦ ❦ ❦ ❦ ❦ ❦ ❦ ❦

✌ GIVE YOUR ✌
PRAYERS WINGS

Trust would settle every problem now.
— A Course in Miracles

It is important to know how and when to pray, but it is equally important to know how and when to *stop* praying. It is not true that the more you pray, the greater your chances of your prayers being answered. As in all arts, sciences, and disciplines, prayer has a point of diminishing return; success is not a matter of working harder—it is about working *smarter*. You cannot truly claim to have mastered the art of prayer until you have mastered the art of *releasing* prayer.

"How could I possibly add to my prayer power by ceasing my praying?" you may rightfully ask. You must release your prayers so God can answer them. It may even be said that the *whole purpose* of prayer is to get to the point where you turn your intentions over to the universe.

Let us review for a moment how prayer works. The part of the mind that prays is the part that is in fear, confusion, or need; you have temporarily forgotten who you are and overlooked the presence of God within you and around you. If you had perfect faith and a perfect awareness of the Presence, you would never need to pray; you would (and will) live in a constant condition of love, joy, and appreciation.

The purpose of prayer is not to change God's mind, which always knows your wholeness and deservingness. The purpose of prayer is to change your mind so you can see through the eyes of God.

Prayer is a unique and wondrous phenomenon that forms a bridge between the separated mind and the whole mind. When you have traversed the gap that doesn't exist, you can relax into serenity and release your concern to the hands of Love. The one who prays has set herself apart from the One Who answers. It is this One to Whom the prayer must be entrusted, for if you knew how to answer your own prayers, you would not be praying in the first place.

Letting your prayers fly is like mailing a letter to a friend across the country. After you have written what you want to communicate, you drop the letter into a mailbox and trust that it will be delivered. You would not stand behind a lamppost and watch to be sure that the mailman picks it up. You would not follow the carrier to the post office and hover over the shoulders of the mail sorters. You would not squat in the back of the mail truck, stow away on the airplane next to the mailbag, and follow the letter through the delivery processes, making sure the letter gets put into the right mailbox. While this scenario sounds ridiculous, it is not unlike attempting to follow your prayer to its natural culmination. In spite of all the jokes about the postal system, nearly every letter gets delivered to the right place in a reasonable time. And that is a human-designed system; consider how much more effective is the divinely designed universal delivery service!

If you are the kind of person who feels that you have to control everything and make sure every detail is handled in the way and time you expect, releasing your prayer could be the most important step in your prayer process. Consider that the pain or fear that has moved you to pray is most likely tied intrinsically to your sense of mistrust. Simply letting go of your prayer will assist you in letting go of the control struggle that led you to pray in the first place.

Prayer must ultimately lead to the awareness that we live in a benevolent universe.

Albert Einstein, one of the most illumined geniuses in history, noted, "There is really only one question that science seeks to answer: *Is the universe a friendly place?"* If the universe is dangerous by nature, you had better stow away in the mail truck and pray forever, for you cannot trust life to take care of you, and you had better do it all yourself. On the other hand, if there is a loving Force operating behind the scenes, you can relax and trust other people and God to help you in ways that you cannot help yourself.

ễ ễ ễ ễ

Holding on to prayer beyond its due time is an affirmation of *lack* of faith and will bear negative results. After you have gotten clear on what you want, affirmed your deservingness to have it, and asked God for help, any more energy you invest will only backfire. When you overpray, you are saying, in effect, "I don't believe that God has heard my request or that He will answer it. So I had better keep badgering Him until I get what I want." Yes,

*Persistence in prayer is good—
but faith is more powerful.*

Jesus noted that "if you had but the faith of a mustard seed, you could move mountains." One good mustard seed of faith in prayer will bear more profound results than dragging a forest of redwoods with a bulldozer.

Remember that...

Prayers are effective for their essence, not volume.

When you get the sense that your prayer has been heard (by you, as well as God) and you feel some relief and empowerment, give thanks and stop. You have done your part; now let God do Hers/His.

☙ ☙ ☙ ☙

Praying or doing an act of faith is like planting a seed. You place the seed gently into the ground, nourish it, water it, cover it with soil, and then you let it be. If you go back and dig up the seed every day to see if it is growing, you will damage it and undermine the results you seek to achieve. Like any embryonic growth, there is a gestation time during which you do not see any obvious results. If your faith is small, you will wonder and worry if your seed is growing. But remember that many growth processes are happening on an invisible level. A human mother sees no visible growth in her womb during the first trimester of pregnancy, while many miraculous changes are occurring! Trust that an invisible Gardener, guided by wisdom, is tending to your seedling even when you cannot see it.

A Course in Miracles tells us, "The presence of fear

is a sure sign that you are trusting in your own strength." Acting or praying anxiously is a sign that you believe it is all up to you. When I saw a statue of the famed Atlas shouldering the earth, I recognized that he was not a happy camper as he struggled with all his might to keep the world from falling. Obviously Atlas was not aware of a Higher Power, which would uphold the universe even in his absence. In prayer and all of life, a certain amount is up to you, and a certain amount is up to God. A great deal of prayer wisdom is the recognition of what belongs to *you,* and what belongs to Spirit.

Like the classic symbol of Sagittarius, we must point our arrow in the direction of our dreams and let it fly. Once you have visioned and acted, step back and allow the universe to support you. God will create miracles, but you must leave space for them. Let go and let God. You do not have to do it all yourself, and you are not asked to. Plant your seed, and trust that it is in good hands.

Envision with perfect intention,
then let go with perfect faith.

❦ ❦ ❦ ❦

I lovingly place my prayers in Your hands, God. I have declared my intentions with a whole heart, and now I release them so You can fulfill them. I recognize that manifestation is a glorious co-creative process in which I do my part and You do Yours. I trust You to take care of what I cannot, and I give up any sense of anxiety, resting secure in the comfort of Your strength. I offer my visions to the magnificent, invisible power that brings forth healing in miraculous ways. I let go and let God.

❦ ❦ ❦ ❦ ❦ ❦ ❦ ❦

✌ PRAYING FOR KEEPS ✌

Do not give to dogs what is holy,
and neither cast pearls before swine.
—Jesus Christ

One of the strangest instructions Jesus gave to one he healed was, *"Now go home and tell no one."* Why would he give such odd advice?

Jesus was a master metaphysician. He understood the power of thought and the internal dynamics of the subconscious. Jesus knew that for the healing to be sustained, the recipient would have to maintain the healing consciousness after he left Jesus' presence. So the master advised the patient not to cast his pearl (the spiritual experience of healing), before swine (the limiting thoughts of cynical minds).

Perhaps you have had this disgruntling experience: You underwent a significant event that touched or changed you, and then, in your emotionally vulnerable state, you told someone who did not share the same enthusiasm and who undermined your good news. "Oh, I know someone that happened to," your less-then-helpful friend responded. "It didn't last; it was a fake."

Suddenly you felt deflated, confused, and you may have begun to doubt yourself or your experience. In your sensitivity, you succumbed to the doubter's negative influence. You would have done better, you realize in retrospect, to just keep your mouth shut.

Another variation on this theme is to tell someone about an important project or dream in a seminal state. You come up with a unique idea, and you go to the wrong person to explain it or ask for support. "That will never work," she says, "lots of people have tried that, they couldn't do it, and I don't see how you will." Shot down again.

We must exercise discernment when choosing those to whom we communicate our spiritual experiences and newborn ideas. A prayer, like a healing or a vision, is a very intimate and personal experience, and must be purposefully nurtured until it is strong enough to be released to a world that may doubt or challenge it. Like the mother of the embryo we have alluded to, you must lovingly guard your meaningful inner experiences until they have a life of their own.

Imagine a tree newly planted in a field. When the sapling is young, the farmer builds a fence around it so the cattle grazing nearby do not eat or trample it. Then, when the tree has grown to a substantial size, the farmer removes the fence. By that time, the tree is so firm and strong that the cattle can rest in its shade and rub up against it for comfort.

Even though we may be physically mature and intellectually sophisticated, our subconscious is highly suggestible; it takes the impressions that come to it and recreates what it observes. Just as you would protect your sensitive child from adverse influences, you must shield your subconscious from impressions that would detract from your well-being. Whenever you read a newspaper, watch a violent movie or television show, get involved in fear-based stories, or speak of your shortcomings or those of others, you are feeding poison to your subconscious. Every thought we think—especially when accompanied by an emotion—will manifest in some way, such as in the dream world we enter at night. Since we are always in the process of creating, we must take care to digest the most nutritious thoughts and images possible. The question is not, "Do you create?" but "*What* do you create?"

Of all that we do, our prayer life requires the most nurturing, for in it we summon the power of God to build the life we would choose. Do not broadcast your prayer intentions to everyone you meet; that will not give them power. Tell your prayers only to a few close friends whom you know will support and empower them to come true. One or two good prayer partners is all you need. *To build your powers of manifestation, match your friendships with your visions.*

If you encounter people who do not support your intentions, it will do you no good to blame or argue with them. If people's comments hurt you, it is only because they are mirroring a thought within you that agrees with them. If such a situation occurs, you can thank the other person (silently) for showing you the area in your belief system that needs strengthening. Then, when you return to your inner sanctuary, do affirmations to override and replace the negative beliefs. Continually purify, upgrade, and remold your subconscious so that it creates what *you* choose, rather than building up the debris others would cast into your holy world.

When your prayer has been answered and you are well established in its manifestation, you may speak of your blessing openly and honor Spirit for assisting you. Then, like the tree that shelters the cattle, others may be inspired by your blessing, and you will serve as a model for success that they may apply to their own intentions.

ॐ ॐ ॐ ॐ

After your initial manifestation, you must continue to sustain your prayer consciousness. I have experienced cases in which I or another person prayed vigorously for a healing or success, and then when the goal began to take form, the person praying complacently fell back into a nonprayerful attitude. You can guess the result: The manifestation began to unravel, or a challenge came forth that required the individual to take up the prayer again.

Jesus instructed us to "pray without ceasing." This does not mean that we are to utter rote prayers all day long; it means that we must sustain the healing consciousness. Consider a man who, after many years of drinking, develops a liver disease. His doctor tells him that if he wants to restore his liver to any degree of health, he must give up alcohol. The fellow becomes alarmed and stays away from liquor. A number of months pass, the patient returns for a checkup, and the doctor gives him the good news that his liver is significantly improved. Heartened by the diagnosis, the man decides to go out and celebrate by having a drink, which leads to further drinking, the return of dis-ease, and the undoing of the health he attained.

The purpose of prayer is not to attain a quick fix and then go back to living in the consciousness that led to our need to pray in the first place. The function of prayer is to lift our soul into a new consciousness, one aligned with our well-being and our soul's purpose, so that our life becomes new. We are not looking for just a boon or a miracle (although those come along the way); we are striving to step into a new outlook that will bring greater clarity and effectiveness to all that we do. We can say that our prayers are effective only when we come to know ourselves and God more intimately, and live in a new energetic vibration.

☙ ☙ ☙ ☙

As a natural extension of our desire to sustain our prayer results, we must support others in sustaining theirs. Be sensitive to the prayer needs of your friends, and speak only words in alignment with their intentions.

I observed my mentor Hilda Charlton teaching a student a caustic lesson. A few minutes after we had prayed for the physical healing of a woman named Karen, another student, Donna, approached Karen and suggested some medicine to help her condition. When Hilda heard about this conversation, she castigated Donna severely. "How dare you undo the healing I just effected!" Hilda rebuked the student. "We finally got Karen into the healing consciousness, and you come along and tell her what she needs to do to get healed! If she is healed, then she is healed, and I don't want you poisoning her mind with things for her to do as if she still needed healing."

Hilda was offering an advanced lesson: If someone you know has chosen a healing path with a doctor or teacher who is taking a particular tack that is working for them, do not attempt to superimpose another method that may undermine the current therapy, confuse the patient, or cast them back into the consciousness of need. *Belief* is the larger portion of healing. (Voltaire noted, "The art of medicine consists of amusing the patient while nature effects the cure.") So, if someone is cultivating a particular belief and doing well with it, don't interfere. If her belief is not working, or she comes to you with a question, then offer what you can. If not, support her in the path she has chosen, rather than trying to superimpose your will. There are many paths to healing, all of which work when applied diligently. Let us honor others as we would wish to be honored.

ॐ ॐ ॐ ॐ

How, then, does the instruction to sustain prayer jive with the principle of releasing prayer and letting God do the rest? Praying is like picking a fruit from a tree. If you pick the fruit before it is ripe, it will be tasteless, without nutrition, and may be poisonous. And if you leave it on the branch after it is ripe, it will become rotten and just as useless. To pick the fruit at the right time, you must watch for the right size, color, and texture, and be aware of the time of the season for harvest.

In prayer, you may let go of attention to a specific need when (1) the result has become so solid that there is no chance of its undoing; (2) you have no further emotional charge on the issue; (3) you feel established in the consciousness your prayers have lifted you attain; and (4) your mind and heart are turned toward new and more expansive things. Even after any or all of these results are accomplished, every so often give thanks for your manifestation.

In the Greek translation of the Bible, from which our English version derives, there is a word that has been grossly mistranslated and misunderstood. Yet the true understanding of this word brings great illumination to our prayer practice. The Greek word *metanoia* is most often translated as "repent." Probably just seeing this word brings shivers to your spine, since it has become a favorite whip of preachers who have linked the word with sin, punishment, and the wrath of God. The actual meaning of *metanoia* has nothing at all to do with sin or punishment; its literal translation is "a transformation of mind," or "a shift in attitude." Such a shift is exactly what we are looking for in prayer. We are seeking to raise our mind above the fears and limits that keep us in mental and emotional chains, and come to see the world through new eyes, in the light of innocence, love, and wholeness. So we can take a powerful but long-bandied Biblical phrase, "Repent, for the Kingdom is at hand!" and bring it into a new and welcome light: "Wake up, for the Love of God is here now, and you can have it!"

🐚 🐚 🐚 🐚

Prayer is not just a tool or a practice; it is an art and a way of life. To pray without ceasing is to keep your mind linked with the infinite power of the universe. Prayer is not a formula, but an attitude; not an obligation, but an opportunity. If, as a child, you were forced to sit for long hours and utter words that were meaningless to you, you were not praying at all (except perhaps to be released from your predicament!). True prayer joins the heart of a human being with the heart of God. The consistent prayer of the heart yields only more and more love, aliveness, health, and peace. Like our old friend E.T., prayer is our medium to phone home and be reunited with the Source that we missed while we wandered in a far country. There is no experience more fulfilling than to be reunited with the peace we once knew, and find that it is with us always.

❧ ❧ ❧ ❧

I give thanks for the wisdom and strength to grow my dreams in the chamber of my heart. I am open and receptive to all the help I can receive from a Higher Power. I release any persons or situations not in harmony with my vision, and I draw unto me those who can support the intentions I choose. Thank you, God, for sustaining me and my prayers, and for growing a healed and whole world from the seed of my visions. May my thoughts and actions ultimately nourish many.

❧ ❧ ❧ ❧ ❧ ❧ ❧

❧ JUST DO IT ❧

Pray devoutly and hammer stoutly.
— English proverb

Every week Daniel prayed to win the lottery. At the end of each week when he did not win, Daniel grumbled that his prayer had not been answered. Finally, after many weeks of missing the jackpot, Daniel angrily stormed the altar of his church, raised his clenched fist, and railed, "If you're such a great God, why don't I have any money? I have been praying for a long time, and I haven't won a dime! If you don't help me win the lottery soon, I'm going to become an atheist!"

Suddenly a great voice boomed from above, "The least you could do, Daniel, is buy a lottery ticket!"

While Daniel came to God with his request, he was not doing his part to assist God. The power of prayer becomes real only when we act on our prayers. When you take a step in the direction of your vision, you demonstrate that you believe in your goal and you are willing to manifest it. Then miracles begin as the universe rallies to support you in a million ways you never could have planned.

In the movie *Jerry Maguire*, Tom Cruise plays a

sports agent who pleads with his client, *"Help me help you."* God, our ultimate agent, needs our help to help us. Comic Sam Levinson quipped, "The helping hand you have been looking for is at the end of your own arm." Cardinal Spellman advised, "Pray as if all depends on God, and act as if all depends on you." Your actions give form to the chalice that God will fill.

Your dreams are worthy of your efforts. Do not be put off by statistics, fear, or the negativity of others. The earth is a place where we grow spiritual muscles by *participating in the adventure.* Don't worry about failing; even if the vision doesn't turn out as you expect, at least you know you gave it your all. The only real failure is not trying.

Life is not about having gifts dropped in our lap; it is about claiming our power as co-creators with God. Don't expect God to generate your life for you; expect God to help you create your vision. Then, as you become responsible for your own success, you enter into a small group of dedicated souls the world names "masters."

ॐ ॐ ॐ ॐ

Most important prayers require a *leap of faith.* To move ahead, you must let go of the world you have equated with security, and step into uncharted territory. At some point you inevitably find yourself hesitating on the brink of the unknown, wondering whether you are divinely inspired, or just crazy. Behind you lies the past, which is no longer acceptable, and ahead of you lies a questionable future. "What shall I do now?" you wonder.

Go to your video store and rent the film *Indiana Jones and the Last Crusade.* At the climax of the movie, after Indy has endured all manner of trials and ordeals in his search for the Chalice of Christ, he finds himself on the precipice of a bottomless chasm. On the other side of the abyss is the temple where the Holy Grail awaits. Indy looks down and sees no possible way to cross the pit. Then he remembers the advice given him about what he must remember when he reaches his last test: *Faith.* Indiana draws a deep breath, releases his foothold on the ledge, and steps out onto the chasm, with no apparent means of support. Then a miracle happens: As he leans out onto nothingness, a bridge appears under Indy's foot, and suddenly he has the support he needs— his step activated it. Soon Indy retrieves the Grail and carries it to the lips of his dying father, whose life is saved by drinking from the sacred cup.

This scene is a metaphor for all leaps of faith: You must step forward with total trust in the unseen God. If you wait until you are sure of success, it will be too late—and you will miss out on the whole purpose of your test, which was to develop your muscle of confidence in yourself and an unseen Power.

Only those who see the invisible
can do the impossible.

If you know how you will accomplish your mission, faith is not required. But if you do not know how you will achieve your goal and you forge ahead anyway, you are mobilizing faith, which magnetizes the mightiest results. "Blessed are those who have seen and believe; even more blessed are you who have not seen, and yet believe."

Faith is made real only by acting on it. You cannot claim that you have faith unless you are simultaneously *doing*. It takes great courage to move ahead when you don't know *how* your dream will come true, but that it *will*. Acts of trust in God are rewarded in proportion to the leap of faith you take to achieve them; long shots pay the highest return. Your investment is belief, and God's response is a miracle. The happiest people I know are those whose leaps of faith have landed them on higher ground. Through experience they have proven the existence of a Higher Power that will help us if we but ask. Think big—settle for more.

୬ ୬ ୬ ୬

The people who have changed the world—beginning with their own lives—were not just thinkers, but *doers*. "To know, and not to do, is not to know." Many are those who have talked truth, yet few are those who have lived it.

All of the changes occurring in our lives and the world around us are urging us to dig into the deepest place of faith within us, and act from our strength, not our fear. You and I have chosen to be on this planet at this exciting and critical time, to draw forth our true spiritual power and bring the world into alignment with the light. Such a bold adventure requires us to step into the darkness so that we can illuminate it. Many old and unconscious internal programs are bubbling to the surface now, for the purpose of healing. To accomplish our mission, we must think with the mind of God, love with the heart of God, and act with the strength of God. Your destiny is a glorious one, and it is time to claim it.

The best way to predict the future

is to create it.

❧ ❧ ❧ ❧

Help me to walk my talk. Make my life meaningful by my actions. Give me the faith to walk hand in hand with Spirit, and to prove the presence of God by my deeds. I can do anything I set my mind and heart to do, for I do not walk alone. Thank you, God, for being my steadfast and stalwart companion. With You by my side, nothing is impossible, and the universe opens its treasures to me.

❧ ❧ ❧ ❧ ❧ ❧ ❧ ❧

✤ TRUTH AND ✤
APPEARANCES

Judge not by appearances,
but judge with righteous judgment.
—Jesus Christ

I had the pleasure of meeting Alberto Aguas, a handsome Brazilian shaman with the gift of healing. I saw Alberto lay hands on several patients, to the accompaniment of soaring classical music. I felt honored to watch this dedicated healer move intuitively, his hands and entire body guided by an unseen yet very obvious force.

During a class, Alberto told us, "I performed two of my most powerful healings on patients who passed on not long afterward."

"How could that be?" a student asked.

"The purpose of healing is not necessarily to bring about a certain physical condition," Alberto explained. "Sometimes its purpose is to bring a soul to peace. The patients I just described had, on a deeper level, chosen to leave this world. In the process they needed to find resolution and freedom within themselves. I can tell when a patient receives healing; I experience a kind of psychic "clicking" during which tumblers seem to fall in place. I felt that sense of deep resolution with these patients; the fact that they passed on is secondary to the fact that they found inner peace."

Like healing, we cannot judge the effects of our prayer by outer circumstances. We must remember that our prayers always have power and that, if the recipient is open to receiving our blessings, he or she will. Because prayer is based on scientific universal law, *all prayer has an effect.* Sometimes, however, the effects are not observable, and sometimes the answers to our prayers do not come in a form we expect or understand. We must have faith that our thoughts and intentions are contributing to the well-being of the one for whom they are intended. When assessing prayer, we must depend on spiritual vision rather than worldly observation.

We must always honor the free will of the person for whom we are praying. While you may deeply desire the healing of a loved one and you pray diligently for their wellness, ultimately it is their choice that will determine their results. Just as you would not like anyone else to have the power to choose for you, you do not have the right or the ability to choose for another. If you are praying for loved ones and they do not seem to be responding, remember that their soul is choosing this experience, though it be difficult, to learn a valuable lesson they would not be able to master if you could lift the circumstances from them. Perhaps they have chosen to build certain spiritual muscles through the experience, and if you removed it from them they would not have the opportunity to grow. We cannot know the deeper inner purpose of someone else's life choices; we can only love them and hold the vision of their inner beauty and wholeness. If you pray for someone and your desired results do not come about in the way and time you would like, do not try to force your will. Continue to hold their best interests at heart, and lovingly release them with the faith that they are in God's hands, and ultimately their well-being will shine forth.

You cannot fail at prayer. Every prayer spoken with a whole heart and meaningful intention must change the universe, beginning with yourself. Prayer is your lifeline to your Source. Imagine a deep-sea diver in an old-fashioned diving suit, breathing through a long tube to a source of oxygen above the surface of the ocean. In a like manner, we are spiritual beings going through an adventure on earth. Though we live and play in the world, we will never be satisfied with material rewards only. We need to feed our soul regularly. Prayer and meditation are our ways of tapping into the deepest ground of our being, and drawing sustenance from the light that we are. Look not to the outside world to give you what only Spirit can provide. And Spirit *will* provide.

🐦 🐦 🐦 🐦

Today I see with the eyes of God. I lift my vision from the mortal, the frail, and the false, and focus on the truth of eternal love. I am not deluded by the shadows of earth; I look upward and inward, and with my spiritual eye I behold a universe of infinite good. I release my loved ones to the hands of God and I trust. I know that all of my prayers reach heaven because heaven is my birthright and my God welcomes me home.

🐦 🐦 🐦 🐦 🐦 🐦 🐦 🐦

THE TECHNIQUE OF PRAYER

Prayer is spiritual in nature and scientific in practice. If you follow certain simple steps, you will find the peace that surpasses understanding and manifest the joy and healing you seek.

Below is a proven and effective prayer technique. There are many routes to the mountaintop, and each of us must find the way that works best for us. I have been using this method for many years, and through it I have experienced deep wholeness and the awareness of the presence of God. I offer this technique to you with the hope and faith that you, too, shall enjoy the lasting benefits of true prayer from the heart.

The Environment of Prayer

While you can pray anywhere at any time (and real prayer leads to praying without ceasing), you can bolster your practice by creating an atmosphere conducive to prayer. Establish an altar area in your home. Dedicate a room, section of a room, or at least a small table area as your altar. Choose a locale away from the activities of daily life, such as watching television, work, eating, or normal conversation. The purpose of your altar is to build an energy that reminds you of God and brings you peace. Just as we decorate our home with photographs and art that remind us of people and things we love, the altar lifts our thoughts to the divine.

Adorn your altar with symbols of God, peace, and healing. Place photos or likenesses of divine beings, saints, cherished spiritual teachers, or loved ones on it. Add a candle, Bible, incense, flowers, crystals, sacred stones, feathers, or any inspiring object you feel empowered to behold. Your altar is your own personal creation and should be meaningful to you.

Keep your altar area meticulously clean, and do not allow junk or worldly activities to infringe on your sacred space. Do your prayer, meditation, chanting, or uplifting reading in this area so it builds up a healing vibration, and the moment you enter the area you feel peaceful. God lives in your home always, and the altar is the place that mirrors this Presence.

Regular Practice

Prayer is a skill that you attain only by consistent practice. If you pray only when you feel like it or when it's convenient or when you're in a jam, you will not build the spiritual muscles to go down deep and find true meaning. While regularity may at first require discipline, eventually it becomes easy, joyful, and extremely desirable.

Begin each day with prayer. We know that the first five years of a child's life are the formative years; the impressions the child receives during that period strike the keynote for his or her life. Likewise, the first minutes of your day set the tone for your entire day. You can choose the kind of day you will have, but you must *choose it before your day begins.* If you get involved in busy-ness, work, or conversation the moment you get up, it will be more difficult to set your tone for your day. If you have a family, or obligations you must attend to upon awakening, then do so, but find time to be with God at the first opportunity. If you can rise a half hour before your family, you will find that that small effort is greatly rewarded.

How long should you pray? I have found that 20 minutes is the minimum time to settle my mind and find the quiet place within me. If you are just starting out and 20 minutes seems burdensome, start with five and work your way up. If you are praying correctly, you will want to stay with it and enjoy its benefits; some days you may sit for an hour. You will know.

When should you stop praying? When you feel complete, as if you have had a good meal for the soul; and you feel nourished, whole, and positive. Stop praying if you feel agitated or uncomfortable for more than a few minutes. It is not unusual for a sense of jitteriness to come up in prayer or meditation. Often if you take some deep breaths and refocus, the discomfort will pass. But if uneasiness continues, do not fight with yourself. It is time to stop. Most of the time you will conclude your prayer in a feeling of deep well-being.

Pray also before going to sleep. The transition between waking and sleeping is as important as waking up in the morning. When we sleep, we step into another dimension in which we do important inner spiritual work. If you go to sleep in a state of agitation or hyper-stimulation, you will spend a great deal of your night working out the unrest you brought into sleep, and you will not enjoy the spiritual renewal sleep serves to provide. Prayer or meditation before sleep will assist you in clearing any unresolved traumas from your day and prepare you to enter a positive sleep state, from which you will awaken refreshed and renewed. You will also need less sleep.

Do not watch the news or disturbing movies before you sleep, and do not get into an argument with your spouse. If an issue comes up, do your best to handle it quietly and peacefully or table it until tomorrow. The refreshment you feel from a good night's sleep preceded by prayer will put you in a far better position to resolve any issues you must face.

In the evening, 20 minutes would also be a good amount of time to pray, meditate, read uplifting words, or listen to soothing music. If you are very tired, then just sit quietly for a few moments and remember God. Thank the Source of Love for your day and invite It to be with you in your sleep. God does not live in time; She feels intentions more than words.

Relaxation

To set the stage for prayer or meditation, come into a relaxed state. Close your eyes, take several long deep breaths, and systematically relax the parts of your body, from your feet to the top of your head. Listen to soothing music if you like. A practice such as yoga, tai chi, or exercise will assist you in unwinding beforehand. Any method that brings you ease and peace is helpful.

I do not recommend lying down while you pray or meditate. Such a position is conducive to falling asleep, which (although it has its benefits) does not provide the conscious focus of meditation. There is also the likelihood of drifting off into a psychic plane that is neither sleep nor meditation. The recommended posture for meditation is sitting upright with a straight spine.

Once your prayer session begins, keep your body still and do not give in to distractions. Try not to wiggle or scratch, and do not get up to go to the bathroom or answer the phone unless it is absolutely necessary. Staying with your practice will bring you very strong focus, which will create a space for you to find the deepest peace in your soul.

Concentration

Begin your session with a few moments of concentration. Gaze at the flame of a candle, observe your breath, or say a mantra or affirmation. This will remove your attention from a million little thoughts and distractions, and put you on the inward path with resolve.

Contemplation

Take an uplifting thought and let it ruminate in your mind so it lifts you into the consciousness of the divine.

Affirmations such as "The peace of God is shining in me now"; "All things are working together for good"; or "I am the beloved Child of God, perfect, free, and whole" will sink deep into your subconscious, remind you of the truth, and reprogram negative imprinting. Any idea that brings you joy and happiness is a good one to digest.

This is a good time for you to talk to God. Develop a personal relationship with your Creator, and speak to Him or Her as a beloved friend. Tell Spirit what is going on in your mind and heart, ask for support and help, and give thanks for the love and beauty in your life. Your words will be heard. After you have spoken, listen for God's response. It will come.

If you are so inclined, engage in creative visualization. Imagine a beautiful nature scene and mentally place yourself into it. See the green of the trees, smell the scent of the flowers, hear the rhythmic lullaby of the waves lapping on the shore, and bask in the brightness of the sun. Picture yourself with optimum health, great relationships, an ideal level of prosperity, and a positive frame of mind. Invite Jesus or any other beloved teacher to meet you; sit down under a tree with him and have an intimate conversation. The more you visualize, the more real your peaceful world will become, and you will thrill to go to your inner sanctuary. (I have produced two recordings of guided imagery: *Peace* and *Journey to the Center of the Heart*, designed to guide listeners on an inner voyage. To order, see the introductory pages of this book.)

Another practice you will enjoy is reciting a meaningful prayer or psalm. Rather than simply mouthing rote words, take each line, such as "Our Father Who art in heaven" and feel the inner meaning of the verse. Get a sense of what the speaker was feeling when he uttered it. Discover the power of the prayer—not through the eyes and words of others—but within your own heart.

Meditation

After you feel inspired and soul-filled, let go of the words and rest in the golden silence. Here you will find perfect peace that words cannot speak. Let go of aspiring *toward* God, and become *one* with God. In this moment beyond time, questions dissolve, and all becomes clear.

Thoughts may arise during your meditation time, but do not sit down to tea with them. Consider thoughts to be like clouds drifting by on a spring day; do not fight them, but don't engage with them either. You will discover that you are much more than your passing thoughts, and your true nature is far richer than anything your senses experience. Even a few moments with God in the golden silence is the gift of a lifetime. To touch God each day will fulfill you in ways that the world cannot.

Blessing

After you have basked in peace to your heart's content, take your positive energy and radiate it to the world. Roll out a golden carpet of love to prepare the way for your day, and invite all of your good to come to you in the right way and in the perfect time. If you are intent on healing or improving a particular aspect of your life, fill that scene with white light, and thank God for establishing it in ideal harmony and balance. Hold in mind others for whom you are praying, and enfold them in your vision of wholeness. Do not get caught up in the problem, but apply the healing consciousness to such persons and situations. Then broadcast love, blessings, and good wishes to all living things everywhere, and recognize the presence of God in all places at all times.

∞ A PRAYER FOR YOU ∞

Before he left this world, Jesus promised, "I am with you always," and later, "I will never leave you comfortless." He was speaking not as a human being, but as a living spirit. That living spirit is available to you and me at all times, and prayer is our way to reach it.

I pray that all of your most cherished dreams and visions come true. I pray that your heart's desires are fulfilled in miraculous and wonderful ways. I pray that your life is free of fear and pain and that all you do is a blessing to everyone you meet. I pray that God be with you, and that you are continually aware of the Divine Presence.

Even more, I pray that you discover and master the power of prayer; that you come to know your spiritual source so intimately that you experience the deep joy of knowing that the God that created you, walks with you and will never desert you.

All is well. We are not alone, and heaven is within our reach.

❦ ❦ ❦ ❦ ❦ ❦ ❦ ❦

ABOUT THE AUTHOR

Alan Cohen is the author of 13 popular inspirational books, including the classic *The Dragon Doesn't Live Here Anymore* and the award-winning *A Deep Breath of Life*. *The Celestine Prophecy* author James Redfield calls Alan "the most eloquent spokesman of the heart." Alan's column "From the Heart" appears in many new thought magazines internationally, and he is a contributing writer for the *New York Times* bestselling series, *Chicken Soup for the Soul*.

Alan resides in Maui, Hawaii, where he conducts seminars on spiritual awakening and visionary living. The Mastery Training is a highly focused small-group experience for individuals seeking to bring greater authenticity, love, and integrity to their chosen goals; and add richer aliveness to their work, relationships, and spiritual path. Alan also keynotes and presents workshops at many conferences and expos throughout the United States and abroad.

For a free catalog of Alan's books, audiocassettes, and video, or to receive his newsletter including a listing of upcoming seminars in your area, call (800) 462-3013, or write to the Publicity Director at Hay House, Inc., P.O. Box 5100, Carlsbad, CA 92018-5100.

To write to Alan Cohen directly or receive more detailed information about his Mastery Training in Hawaii, write to Alan Cohen Programs, 430 Kukuna Road, Haiku, Hawaii, 96708, or call (800)568-3079. Visit Alan Cohen's Website at **www.alancohen.com.**

❧ ❧ ❧ ❧ ❧ ❧ ❧ ❧

We hope you enjoyed this Hay House
book. If you would like to receive a free
catalog featuring additional Hay House
books and products, or if you would
like information about the Hay
Foundation, please contact:

Hay House, Inc.
P.O. Box 5100
Carlsbad, CA 92018-5100

(800) 654-5126
(800) 650-5115 (fax)

❧ ❧ ❧ ❧ ❧ ❧ ❧ ❧

Please visit the Hay House Website at:
www.hayhouse.com

Busy
448 . 65168